AN ADVOCATE'S TALE

the memoirs of
Lord Brand

SCOTTISH CULTURAL PRESS

First published 1995
Scottish Cultural Press
PO Box 106, Aberdeen AB9 8ZE
Tel: 01224 583777
Fax: 01224 575337

British Library Cataloguing in Publication Data
A catalogue record for this book is available from the British Library

ISBN: 1 898218 08 0

Printed and bound by Bookcraft, Midsomer Norton, Bath

A legal Aeneid dedicated with affection and respect to the Right Honourable the Lord Hope of Craighead, Lord President of the Court of Session and Lord Justice-General of Scotland, without whose encouragement and instructive comments it would not have been written, and also to the members of the Faculty of Advocates without whose generous support the author would never have reached a shore.

Forsan et haec olim meminisse juvabit
Perhaps one day it will help to remember even these things
Virgil: *Aeneid* Book 1

Contents

Introduction   vii

Acknowledgements   viii

I   Origins and Childhood (1923-1942)   1

II   Under Arms (1942-1946)   11

III The Post-War Student (1946-1948)   26

IV Stuff Gown (1948-1959)   29

V   Silk (1959-1972)   53

VI Sheriff of Dumfries and Galloway (1968-1970)   59

VII Solicitor General for Scotland (1970-1972)   63

VIII Outer House Judge (1972-1984)   70

IX Inner House Judge (1984-1989)   78

X   Criminal Trials   82

XI *Laudator temporis acti*   86

XII Postscript   90

Appendix: 'An oration to the memory of Robert
Louis Stevenson'   93

Index   102

Introduction

David Brand is one of a distinguished generation of advocates who served their country in both war and peace. Throughout a full life, as soldier, lawyer, husband and father, he has exemplified the best ideals of duty and of devotion to family and faith.

David has always been a popular figure in Parliament House. In his days as a Silk he passed the sternest test of all: he was a favourite of the junior Bar. Many of his younger colleagues have reason to be grateful for his encouragement and generous advice. In his years on the Bench he has adapted with his usual resilience to changes in the profession that cannot always have been to his liking.

This is an account of a successful career that culminated in seventeen years of judicial achievement; but there is much more to David than his eminent contribution to the law. Over many years he has shown to a wide circle of friends his most endearing qualities: humanity, a committed approach to the enjoyment of life and an incurable propensity to reminisce. In these short memoirs there is much for readers to enjoy. There are many more anecdotes that the author's own good nature has led him to withhold. Fortunately, these have already been committed to the oral tradition of the Bar.

In his days of retirement, but not of inactivity, David is blessed with the unfailing support of his devoted wife Vera. On behalf of their friends I wish David and Vera many more years in which to delight us with their company.

Brian Gill

Acknowledgements

In writing these recollections I have been greatly assisted by the Right Honourable the Lord Emslie who lent me his copy of *Faculty Tales* compiled by the late Sheriff R J Wallace, DL. To the Honourable Lord Cameron, KT, DSC, I am deeply indebted, not only for allowing me to reproduce the transcript of his oration at the Stevenson Centenary Dinner, but also for much valuable information which had been preserved in his long memory.

I must also record that, without the diligent assistance and recovery of records carried out by Mr William Howard, formerly a Clerk of Justiciary, it would have been impossible to write considerable parts of these recollections. To each of these gentlemen I express my profound thanks. While disavowing any claim to the scholarship and elegance of the late Monsignor R A Knox, I must acknowledge that the format was inspired by his Spiritual Aeneid.

Finally, I must record my unbounded debt to Professor D A O Edward, CMG, QC, Judge of the European Court of Justice, for his generous reading of the whole of the text and for his valuable criticisms and encouragement, and to the Honourable Lord Gill, formerly the Keeper of the Advocates' Library, for his wise advice on the mechanics of publication and for writing the introduction.

Notwithstanding all the assistance I have received, the imperfections and inaccuracies of the text are wholly mine.

I   *Origins and Childhood (1923-1942)*

Home (1923-1932)

During the last 50 to 60 years journalism has displayed a declining interest in publishing knowledgeable, instructive and elegant obituaries. Presumably they are no longer considered an important 'draw' for advertising revenue. In my youth every paper from the humblest local news-sheet to *The Thunderer* invariably devoted several columns to well-informed obituary articles, relating not only to those who had been famous or notorious but also to a wide variety of the recently dead whose lives, although not colourful, might provide pegs on which to hang a discussion of topics of interest. Thus it was that when my father, who had been Sheriff-substitute of Dumfries and Galloway at Dumfries, died in 1933, an obituarist took the opportunity to quote the following from an article in the *Times Literary Supplement*:

> Probably no judge is brought more closely into contact with the life of the people than a sheriff-substitute in Scotland. He resides among them and, as the local representative of the law, is expected to take a leading part in the social as well as in the official life of his Sheriffdom. He has no exact counterpart in England; for, unlike a County Court judge, he has a practically unlimited civil jurisdiction of first instance, while he has also important duties as a criminal judge and as an administrator.

Since that article was written legislative changes have been made affecting both the Sheriff Courts in Scotland and the English County Courts. The archaic official title of 'sheriff-substitute' has been altered to 'sheriff' to conform to what had been the common usage for many years and the number of sheriffs has been greatly increased. In my father's time each Sheriff Court, apart from those in the cities, was served by one resident sheriff. In a few cases a sheriff sat in more than one court in a Sheriffdom. There are now only one or two courts in the entire country which are not served by more than one sheriff. The increase in the volume of business has made the change inevitable but I fear that the multiplication in the number of sheriffs has made the office less personal and tended towards anonymity.

In retrospect our days in Dumfries seem to have been idyllic. We had an agreeable house, Huntingdon, on the Moffat Road with grounds which provided ample scope for my brothers and myself to roam and pursue our interests. I developed a keen interest in farming through the kindness of the Lindsays of Clumpton whom my father employed to cultivate our paddock. They gave me a warm welcome on my frequent excursions by bicycle to their farm on the Lockerbie Road where Mrs Lindsay took it for granted that I would share the very generous meals which she provided. In those days there were no milking machines or, for that matter, mechanically propelled machinery of any kind. Anyone available was expected to take a hand in the milking. I was only too cager to offer my services and, consequently, became a competent milker before being dispatched to my prep school. As milking time approached, a collie was sent from the farm steading to bring the milk herd in from over the hill. When the cattle reached the entrance to the steading the gate was opened and each cow went to her customary stall in the byre. I loved my all too brief farming days and all the livestock from Rosie, the massive Clydesdale mare, who did the heavy work, to tiny pups and chicks. It never occurred to me to want to be a fireman or an engine driver. I enjoyed an easy rapport with the farming community and their livestock which I assumed would continue indefinitely. Alas! my father concluded that I ought to be subjected to a more intensive intellectual training than was to be acquired merely by extending my considerable bucolic vocabulary and I was dispatched to Hodder Place where my initial sensation was, inevitably, one of claustrophobia. At Huntingdon my brother Willie kept ducks and tumbler pigeons. Harry, the youngest, was the most self-contained and occasionally got lost in the trees and bushes between the house and what had been the stable and coach-house and was then a garage. I kept a small flock of bantams. In summer the countryside and the villages of the Solway Firth and Galloway were a source of endless pleasure. In a cold winter the colour and excitement of the bonspiel at Lochmaben provided a contrasting thrill. The bonspiel was a curling match on a large

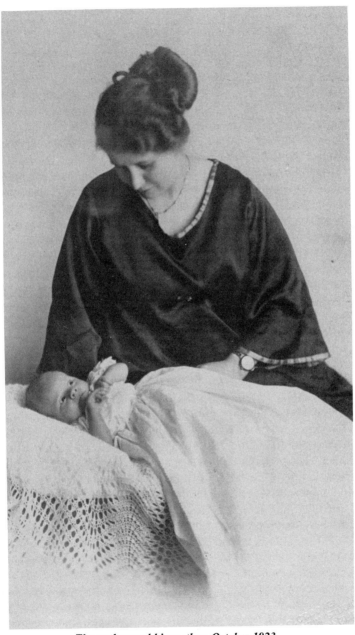

The author and his mother, October 1923

scale. To a small boy the loch was very extensive and fully capable of accommodating the large number of curlers.

My father had been appointed sheriff-substitute at Dumfries in 1925. Before that we lived at 2 Randolph Place, Edinburgh where I was born on 21 October 1923. I was my father's fourth son but the eldest by his second marriage to Frances Bull. My father, James Gordon Brand, was born on 11 June 1872 at the Whitehouse, Whitehouse Loan, Edinburgh. His first wife was Mabel Thomas who died in 1916, survived by her three sons, Stanley, Francis and Clement. My parents were married in North Berwick 25 September 1922, the officiating priest being Father John Gray, whose nephew, Gordon, was subsequently to become the Cardinal Archbishop of St Andrews and Edinburgh. The Archbishop officiated at the marriage of Vera and myself in his Chapel of St Bennets at 42 Greenhill Gardens, Edinburgh, on 7 April 1969.

So far as family history discloses, the Brands all came from Fordoun and Auchenblae in Kincardineshire. According to some scholars, the name is of Norse origin. I prefer the simpler Scots explanation that it was descriptive of the occupation of the bearer of the name, namely that he was a sort of exciseman who was responsible for the branding of casks of liquor to certify their contents. The names of Brand and Brander were not uncommon in Aberdeenshire and Kincardineshire in the days when members of the same community with a common name were distinguished by a suffix derived from their occupation, eg. Miller, which is now to be found in some families as the second half of a double-barrelled name. According to my grandfather, James Brand, the graves of all his forebears were to be found in the kirkyard at Glenbervie. They were all 'Episcopals and non-jurors' and one of them proclaimed Bonnie Prince Charlie at the Mercat Cross at Fordoun. My great-grandfather, Charles Brand, founded the firm of Charles Brand & Son, Civil Engineering Contractors. He lived in Montrose when my grandfather was born but was subsequently the tenant of Fordoun Mains on the Arbuthnott Estate which provided the many horses which were required for the construction of the railways and bridges which his firm undertook. The firm was carried on by my grandfather and thereafter by his son-in-law Donald Arbuthnott and by his sons Harry and Clement.

Although my father was the eldest surviving son, he took no part in the family firm. The eldest son was Charles who was physically handicapped and died young. My father was called to the Scots Bar in 1908, having previously been a Writer to the Signet and, briefly, a partner in the firm of Charles George & Brand, W.S. At the time of his call the Dean of Faculty was William Campbell, K.C., subsequently Lord Skerrington. Professor Candlish Henderson, K.C., a reliable authority, told me that Skerrington had 'a very subtle mind'. Another authority, Major W M Campbell of the Camerons with whom I served in Burma, a very brave man, who was a grandson of the judge, told me that Skerrington was the only man whom he had feared! Skerrington lived at 12 Randolph Crescent which was just round the corner from our house. He appears to have been an aristocrat of exacting standards but got on well with my father with whom he collaborated as co-trustee on a charitable trust. He had a daughter, Gladys, an imperious horsewoman, who stabled her pony in Randolph Lane.

In Dumfries I gradually became conscious of the nature of my father's work. The courthouse in Buccleuch Street, where I sat as sheriff principal from 1968 to 1970, became familiar to me as a small boy. Its main entrance was adorned with Locharbriggs sandstone carved, appropriately, in the shape of a rope! I was allowed to visit my father in his Chambers but not to enter the court room while business was in progress. I became familiar with the bundles of papers tied with pink tape on which he worked at home. Although I was only nine years of age when my father died, his influence on me was profound. He was deeply conscientious and regularly returned to Dumfries from Gullane where we spent the holidays to take the Vacation Courts himself instead of leaving them to be taken by an honorary sheriff. When my father took me walking in Dumfries I was impressed by the amiable respect with which he was greeted by so many of the people. This impression was confirmed by his obituary in the Dumfries and Galloway Courier and Herald which concluded: 'Among the general community also Sheriff Brand's genial and unobtrusive manner made him greatly esteemed'.

While we lived in Dumfries I began to appreciate the camaraderie of my father's brethren of the Bar who called on us when they had occasion to visit the town. These included Lord Kinross, K.C., the Sheriff Principal whose father had been Lord President of the Court of Session and was raised to the peerage as Baron Kinross. As a host, so it is recorded, Lord President Kinross displayed consummate diplomacy. On observing at a dinner party that one of his guests, having become drunk, had fallen asleep, he rang for his butler and said to him 'Mr— has kindly consented to stay the night'. This may explain why the Lord President's soubriquet was 'the butler'. Lord Moncrieff was a very distinctive figure in Dumfries on his visits as the circuit judge. We used to visit him and his family in North Berwick when we stayed at Scotcrest, my father's house in Gullane. He was an outstandingly courteous man but even his informal conversation was notably concise and exacting. In court counsel found his rapid and penetrating questions alarming. Another visitor was John Carmont, who was then at the height of his very considerable powers at the Bar. He had his roots in Dumfries. His elder brother, Canon Carmont, was the parish priest at Annan. I was greatly impressed on being told that Carmont earned 50 guineas a day, a fortune in those days. Our most frequent visitor was Robert Maxwell (subsequently Maxwell-Witham of Kirkconnell) who had been a friend of my father since their student days when they shared lodgings at Greenhill in Edinburgh. Robert Maxwell practised as a solicitor in Dumfries until he became the laird of Kirkconnell near New Abbey following the death of Colonel Maxwell-Witham.

The influence which my father had on me was nurtured and reinforced by my mother who kept his memory alive as an ideal for my brothers and myself to emulate. There was thus engendered in me a growing determination to go to the Bar.

When my father died in 1933 my younger brothers and I did not appreciate the financial inevitability of the disposal of Huntingdon. My mother moved to a house in Braid Road, Morningside, Edinburgh, because it would be convenient to the Benedictine School in Canaan Lane to which my younger brothers could be sent. I was already at Hodder Place, the preparatory school for Stonyhurst. I was followed to Stonyhurst by Willie and Harry. I regretted the return to Edinburgh and the loss of the semi-rural environment which we had enjoyed in Dumfries.

School Days (1932-1940)

I went to Hodder Place in 1932. The school was situated about a mile or so from Stonyhurst beside the river Hodder. Stonyhurst was already part of the family tradition. My father and his brothers as well as my half-brothers and my Brand and other cousins had all been there. Stonyhurst had been founded at St Omers in 1593 to provide Catholic education for English boys because of the Elizabethan penal laws. It was not until 1794 that the college moved to England. Stonyhurst was given to the Jesuits by Thomas Weld who had inherited the estate from the Shireburns by marriage.

When, in 1935, I went up from Hodder to the College at Stonyhurst, I was very fortunate in having as my class master during the highly formative years from 12 to 14, John Firth, S.J. He was then a scholastic aged about 25-30 years who was doing what was then the traditional two to three years teaching break for Jesuit scholastics between their courses in philosophy and theology. In the Jesuit order a scholastic is a man who has passed through the novitiate and taken vows but has not yet been ordained as a priest. John Firth was not a scholar, such as were his fellow scholastics Bernard Basset and Francis Rae, but his father, Ernest Firth, a retired barrister, had been an un-doubted scholar. Ernest Firth and his wife were most hospitable to me in my early days in the army when they invited me to their house in retirement at Scorton. Ernest found it incompre-hensible that anyone went up to Oxford to read any profane subjects other than Classical Mods and Greats, namely Latin and Greek and philosophy and ancient history. Other subjects, except for those with a mathematical bent, were for recreation or entertainment. John Firth inherited his father's recognition of the educational importance of the classics. He had a strong and distinctive character and the ability to give young boys a thor-ough grounding in Latin and Greek. His love of Stonyhurst was unbounded. He had gone to Hodder as a small boy and spent the greater part of the rest of his life at Stonyhurst. John Firth was an outstanding schoolmaster who was tireless in promoting the interests of his boys both within and outside the classroom. I was blessed with an aptitude for the classics which carried me through school and, in large measure, through University. The classics also taught me to appreciate grammatical English. It was thanks to Firth's ability as a Latin master that I won the Junior Latin Prose Competition ahead of my time sharing the prize with John Waterton, a descendant of Charles Waterton, the famous naturalist, who was a year ahead of me.

During my early years at Stonyhurst the Rector was Father Edward O'Connor. He was a scholar and astronomer and a traditional rector who always wore his biretta – the type of cleric described by Ronnie Knox as 'an awful presence'. He had an high tenor voice which earned him the soubriquet of 'minus' from the boys, 'minus' being briefer and less obviously indelicate than *castratus*.

In my third year at the college my classmaster was Father 'Reggie' O'Connor, one of the most remarkable Stonyhurst characters of this century. I do not know how he acquired the nickname of 'Reggie'. His christian name was in fact Frederick which accorded with his tall aristocratic bearing. Before becoming a Jesuit he had been a Naval Officer. During the 1914-1918 war he was a Chaplain in Allenby's Army. It was said that Allenby set such store by Reggie's qualities that, before ordering an attack, he asked 'Where is Father Reggie?' On receiving the reply 'Here he is, sir', the General rejoined 'Very well, let battle commence'! Between the two world wars Reggie taught at Stonyhurst. As our classmaster, Reggie had overall responsibility for our academic progress but the only subject which he himself taught was French, which he did with skill. At least as effective as his formal teaching were his *obiter dicta* on manners and morals couched in memorable phrases – there were no stern warnings about lack of moral fibre or being bounders or outsiders, whom we might have envied, but humorous derision of 'floating about like a jellyfish' or being 'a filthy booby'.

In consequence of the death in 1940 of my Uncle Clement, who had been paying the school fees of my brothers and myself, and the fact that I had adequate qualifications to enter a University, I left school at the age of 16. This was deplored by the staff at Stonyhurst who had expected me to compete for an Oxford Scholarship. It has always been a cause of regret to me that I missed Oxford but a compensating imponderable factor is that, being impecunious, an Oxford degree might have diverted me from the Bar. Leaving Stonyhurst, to which I owe a life-long debt, was a deep wrench.

Edinburgh University (1940-1942)

In the event I entered Edinburgh University in October 1940, joined the University OTC and enlisted in the army at whatever the minimum age was. I was then told by the military authorities to carry on at the University, obtain Certificate 'B' in the OTC and await further orders. I did as instructed and acquired Certificate 'B', Certificate 'A' having been acquired at Stonyhurst. Apart from enabling me to gain Certificate 'B' and thus direct entry to an Officer Cadet Training Unit without going through the ranks, service in the University OTC was not a useful experience. These certificates were respectively evidence of basic and more advanced proficiency in the military arts.

Between 1940 and 1942 I spent a fairly idle time reading Latin, Greek, Moral Philosophy and Roman Law. The classics that I had learned at Stonyhurst saved me from the necessity of serious work. I blush when I hear my compatriots boasting of the superiority of the Scottish education system. Such a superiority may have existed in the past but in this century the vandals and levellers have had their way to the extent that there is a rising tide of illiteracy which our forebears could not have imagined.

During those two years that I spent in Edinburgh I had the advantage of being introduced to the Parliament House and some of its leading personalities. Innes Wedderburn, W.S., our family solicitor, whose father had been a close friend of my father, introduced me to J R Wardlaw Burnet, K.C., who was then Clerk of the Faculty of Advocates and subsequently Vice-Dean. Burnet was an exceptionally charming and kindly man of scholarly appearance. He had been at Cambridge before studying Scots Law. He invited me to his house in Northumberland Street and encouraged me to come to the Bar. Unhappily he died suddenly within a year or two of our meeting while leading for the defence in a murder trial in Glasgow. Innes also took me into the Second Division of the Court of Session where the legendary Craigie Aitchison was presiding as Lord Justice-Clerk. Although comparatively young, he had not long to live. There are innumerable, almost incredible, stories about Craigie. After presiding over a long trial in Glasgow, Craigie vanished and was eventually found on the Isle of Arran to which he was much attached. The law reports bear witness to his erudition and to his

gift of elegant expression, but he lived dangerously. The late
Arthur Duffes, Q.C., a life-long teetotaller and friend of
Craigie's, told me that Craigie had also been a teetotaller until
he went to the war of 1914-1918, but, Duffes added, he was 'a
dull stick until he started to drink'. In a notorious misprint
Punch referred to Craigie as a 'famous Sottish Judge'. When
asked what he would do about it, Craigie replied 'I'll say
nothing and sit tight'. He was short of stature and rubicund of
countenance. His portrait in the Parliament House 'looking like
Charles II', as Duffes put it, is misleading.

One of my few lasting memories of Edinburgh University
between 1940-1942 is of attending the lectures of A E Taylor,
the famous Platonist. He was the incarnation of the proverbially
eccentric professor. He put on increasing layers of clothing, like
a tramp, without apparently shedding any. In winter his great
coat was overlaid by his academic gown. He only refrained
from smoking when he was actually lecturing. A pipe that was
all too obviously alight was then stuck in a pocket with variable
results. On one occasion he had a cab summoned by his servitor. In those days each professor had his own attendant, known
as his servitor. On the cab's arrival the servitor held the door
open for the professor who stepped in and went straight out the
other side. Taylor was consistently oblivious of the fact that, for
many years, female undergraduates had been admitted to the
University. The 'Good morning, gentlemen' with which he began every lecture provoked much stamping of feet and an apology from the rostrum. The morning lecture was normally followed by coffee and talk in J & R Allan's shop in Chambers
Street. Then some work might be squeezed in at the library of
the Old Quad before the demands of billiards, beer and lunch
were met in the University Union or one of the neighbouring
pubs.

II   *Under Arms (1942-1946)*

Silent enim leges inter arma
Laws are silent midst the clash of arms
Cicero: *Pro Milone IV*

The Officer Cadet – August to December 1942

The summer of 1942 saw my formal entry into the Army proper. This occurred in a manner which not even the pen of the late Evelyn Waugh could have made more ludicrous. Being conscious of my educational limitations, I decided that the infantry was the only branch of the service where I might be able to play a not wholly unacceptable and, preferably, unnoticed part. At Stonyhurst, where membership of the OTC was compulsory, I had acquired Certificate 'A' and that despite the fact that I had avoided most of the rigours of field training by joining the band and learning to play a 'B flat' flute. Idle as I was, I could not avoid gaining at least some advantage from membership of an OTC which annually earned the highest commendation from inspecting generals. The efficiency of the Stonyhurst OTC was due to the zeal of Major (subsequently Lieutenant Colonel) L de C F Robertson and to the professionalism and exacting standards of RSM Barry, late of the Irish Guards. Before coming to Stonyhurst Barry had been the RSM at Sandhurst. There he had achieved fame by bawling across the parade ground 'Cadet Prince Henry, you're idle'. Prince Henry, subsequently Duke of Gloucester, was the third son of King George V. The Stonyhurst OTC band regularly won the band competition at the annual camp. This was due to the musicianship of the Drum-major Instructor who had come from the Coldstream Guards. Quite apart from the OTC, the ethos of Stonyhurst inculcated a pride in the profession of arms. In the refectory we sat beneath the portraits of five old boys who had won the Victoria Cross. Since then two more have been added, namely those of Captain Harold Marcus Ervine-Andrews whose award was gazetted on 30 July 1940, and Captain James Jackman whose posthumous award was gazetted on 31 March 1942.

On completing the army form on which one had to express one's preference for one or other arm of the service, I noticed that there was an organisation called 'Motorised Infantry'. Thinking that this might be an agreeable alternative to the plain infantry and being unaware that it was composed solely of the Rifle Brigade and the King's Royal Rifle Corps, who selected their own officer cadets, I plumped for 'Motorised Infantry'. In due course I received an order to report to an Officer Cadet Training Unit in Andover on a specified date, an order with which I sought to comply. Having allayed the suspicions of a sentry and a guard commander, I was taken to the office of an adjutant, a delightful man. He told me that the OCTU to which I had been instructed to report had moved to the Cavalry Barracks, York, and that I should have been so informed. He then looked up the railway timetable, supplied me with a travel warrant and sent a signal to the barracks in York with instructions that I should be met at 3 or 4 am when my train was due to arrive. My journey went according to plan until I reached York railway station. There I looked about optimistically, not to say naively, for the expected reception party. I spotted only one man in military uniform. Although his dress indicated that he was a motorcycle dispatch rider, I approached him with the absurd inquiry whether he had come to meet me. 'Naw,' he replied, 'Boot w'ere are ye bound for?' 'Cavalry barracks,' I told him. 'Well,' said he, 'I'll be passin' Cavalry barracks. If ye cur to sit on me moodguard, I'll drop ye off at gates.' I promptly accepted the offer and was soon at the gates of the barracks. There my way was barred by a sentry with a fixed bayonet. He conducted me to the guardroom to meet the sergeant of the guard. Unimpressed by my story, the sergeant told me that I would spend the unexpired portion of the night on the floor of the guardroom. On the following morning I was taken to the adjutant who told me that he could not understand what I was doing in the Cavalry Barracks where indeed the OCTU to which I had been ordered to report in Andover was now stationed. As far as he was concerned, I did not exist. He would have to get onto the War House (War Office) to find out what was to be done with me. In the meantime I would just have to wait. The long day wore on. After a few hours I returned to the adjutant for a progress report but he was no wiser. By this time, being as yet unaccustomed to the delays associated with any military movement, I felt frustrated and suggested to the adjutant that, if for the time being, the army had no use for my services, he might be good enough to supply me with another railway warrant so that I could return home until I was required. In due course that was what happened and the night following the discomfort of the guardroom was spent in the comfort of my mother's house. On reaching home I found that a cancellation of my posting to Andover – and consequentially to York – had arrived in my absence together with an instruction to stand fast until I received a further order. In a week or two I received an order to report to an OCTU at Dunbar. This was cancelled before I left home. About one month later I received a posting to 163 OCTU at Heysham Towers, Morecambe. This was not cancelled and, having completed the course at Morecambe, I was commissioned in the Argyll and Sutherland Highlanders in December 1942.

I was very fortunate to do my training at 163 OCTU. The instructing staff were delightful and the locality was agreeable. At weekends I was able to visit John Firth's parents at the Priory, Scorton, mid-way between Lancaster and Preston. One of the instructing staff was Captain David McQueen, a regular officer with the Royal Scots. He was a gallant man who later survived a very severe wound and was decorated with the Distinguished Service Order as a company commander. He retired after the war having attained the rank of brigadier. He now lives in Gullane and it is a pleasure to meet him regularly at Muirfield. Life at Heysham was not arduous. I found that the discipline and training of the Stonyhurst OTC had taught me more than I had realised and certainly made life easier than it was for some of the other cadets. This is not to suggest that, when I was commissioned, I was a good soldier or that I ever became one but only that I apparently satisfied such modest demands as were made of me. I was a bad shot and perfectly useless at assembling and dismantling weapons.

The Argyll Subaltern – December 1942 to December 1943

On being commissioned I was posted to 11th Argylls, then part of 15th (Scottish) Division stationed in Northumberland. The

CO was Lieutenant Colonel F M Elliot, who had gained an MC in the 1914-1918 war and a bar while serving on the North-west Frontier of India between the wars. The second in command was Major E L P (Bob) Slayter – inevitably known by the Jocks as 'Oscar', despite the difference in spelling and the fact that he bore no resemblance of any kind either to the famous aesthete or to the Slater whose conviction for the murder of Miss Gilchrist in Glasgow was ultimately quashed. Bob Slayter had spent a considerable part of his peace-time service in the King's African Rifles on account of impecuniosity. The colonial regiments were a lifeline for regular officers without private means as the cost of living was low and the pay was enhanced by Colonial Allowance. The third regular officer in 11th Argylls was Major R M T Baker-Carr. I heard that before the war ended he expired while Town Major of Philipville. I was very fond of Colonel Elliot (known as 'Frontier Frank') and was sorry when he left us to take command of a brigade in Italy. Bob Slayter was a lovable and generous man. A skilled piper, he was a favourite with the Jocks. I was to meet him again in East Africa and, later, in India when he was commanding the 3/4 KAR in 11th (East African) Division.

Shortly after I joined 11th Argylls, 15th (Scottish) Division was reorganised on the basis that the junior infantry battalion in each brigade would be replaced by an armoured regiment. As 11th Argylls was the junior battalion in our brigade we were relegated to form part of a reserve division in West Lancashire. This happened early in 1943 and marked the beginning of a boring and dispiriting spell. We sent off periodical drafts to re-inforce battalions serving overseas. Frank Elliot was replaced by Lieutenant Colonel J D C Anderson of the Gordons. In between them we were commanded, briefly, by a Lieutenant Colonel from the Camerons. He was a regular officer but had com-manded the Lovat Scouts. In this capacity he had had Shimi Lovat, whom he described as his worst company commander, under his command. One can only assume that this amazing failure to appreciate military qualities was caused by their con-cealment due to Shimi's unconventionality. Bob Slayter was posted to the KAR and was replaced as second-in-command of 11th Argylls by Angus Rose.

Towards the end of 1943 an Army Council Instruction was

Lieutenant, Argyll and Sutherland Highlanders, 1943

circulated which invited officers to volunteer for posting to colonial regiments. I decided to respond and was put on CO's
Orders. When I was marched before Colonel Anderson he asked
me whether I was not happy in the Battalion. I replied that I
was, but bored. This satisfied the Colonel who expressed his
pleasure that I had volunteered.

In December 1943 I went on embarkation leave. On leave in
Edinburgh at the same time was Hugh Gordon, a distant cousin,
who was a chaplain in the 51st (Highland) Division, recently
returned to the United Kingdom to prepare for the invasion of
France. Hugh asked me whether I would be agreeable to be
posted to the 7th Argylls in 51st Division as there was a short-
age of RC officers. There was generally a considerable number
of Catholics among the Jocks of the Argylls. It was therefore
appropriate that a Catholic officer should be available to command the R.C. Church parades. I replied that I would be happy
to join the 7th Argylls but that, as I was already on embarkation
leave pending my departure for a colonial regiment, I thought
his proposal was impracticable. Hugh then confidently asserted
that he would have my posting re-arranged as soon as he returned to 51st Division at the end of his leave. He failed in his
purpose.

The King's African Rifles – January 1944 to September 1946

At nos hinc alii sitientes ibimus Afros
But we from here are to go some to arid Africa
Virgil: *Eclogues* Book I

East Africa

I duly sailed for Mombasa on SS *Cameronia* from the Tail of
the Bank in the Firth of Clyde in January 1944. En route for
Greenock I had to go to the Duke of Wellington's barracks in
Halifax to take over a draft of soldiers. We had to march from
the barracks to the railway station in Halifax. It was a memorable occasion. Belying the name of the barracks, the men were
sappers, many of whom were noticeably drunk but genial and
well behaved. There was no ill-discipline. Having entrained, we
sped northwards and passed through Edinburgh. I wondered
whether this would be my last sight of Edinburgh Castle. When

we reached the port of embarkation on the Clyde we saw two or three soldiers from other drafts being taken on board in manacles. These were the chronic deserters who could not voluntarily face overseas service. They were set at liberty when the ship had sailed. I have been told, and I believe it to be true, that the majority of the men who were put on troopers in this way never subsequently caused any trouble. They had deserted whenever they went on embarkation leave because, until they had joined the service, they had never been beyond the areas of their own homes and had an invincible fear of the unknown.

The *Cameronia* was a large transatlantic liner of the Anchor Line, totally unsuitable for tropical conditions. The Master was an elderly Captain in the Merchant Service and, as we subsequently discovered, was to be the Commodore of the convoy. As we took up station in the Firth of Clyde we became part of an astonishing assembly of vessels. There were ships, naval and mercantile, of every description. The Admiralty must have had extraordinary confidence in our Master to put him in command of this vast and heterogeneous fleet. I would have expected an admiral or, at least, a captain in the Royal Navy to be the Commodore of such a convoy. I recently learned from Lord Hope that his father the late Lieutenant-Colonel A.H.C. Hope, O.B.E., W.S., had had a much deeper knowledge of the *Cameronia* and of the Commodore than I had as he had been O.C. Troops on the *Cameronia* for most of the war and had been twice torpedoed. Lord Hope told me that his father had been a close friend and admirer of the Commodore. As I did not meet Colonel Hope on the voyage to Mombasa, I assume that he was enjoying a spell of leave at that time.

Our voyage began by sailing west into the Atlantic before turning east. Thereafter we made course through the Mediterranean for Port Said, being the first convoy to do so since the re-opening of the Straits of Gibraltar to allied shipping. So far as I know, every ship in the convoy reached its destination unscathed after some diversions to evade hostile submarines – a great tribute to the Commodore. At Port Said our progress was interrupted for a day or two by high winds which were liable to blow the ship against the sides of the Suez Canal until they abated. By this time the size of the convoy was reduced as some vessels had left for other destinations. Passage through the canal and the sweet-water lakes confirmed the accuracy of one's recollections of illustrations in school books and picture postcards of Egyptian scenes. Apart from the evidence provided by the inscriptions and gestures on the canal banks of the modern Egyptian's mastery of English obscenities, one's eyes rested on the timeless sights of natives travelling and working with camels and donkeys and the stately women bearing water pots on their heads. Passage through the Red Sea was acutely uncomfortable owing to the intense heat, the over-crowding and the lack of air-conditioning.

About six weeks after leaving the Clyde we tied up in Kilindini, the port of Mombasa, and were put on a troop train for Nairobi. As the train wound its way up the steep winding escarpment we enjoyed the spectacular vista to the East and the freshening air as our altitude increased. On arrival in Nairobi we were transported by trucks to Langata, a base camp some miles from the city. There we were invited to express our preference for being seconded to the King's African Rifles, the Northern Rhodesia Regiment or the Somaliland Gendarmerie. I opted for the King's African Rifles and had the good fortune to be selected to take a course in Swahili which was run by the army at Kabete, near Nairobi. The course lasted 6 weeks and was run with an efficiency which, I fear, is seldom to be found in our schools and universities. I may be prejudiced since at the end of the course I was awarded a Distinction and this proved to be the only phase of my military career in which I earned an accolade. The course gave me a knowledge of Swahili which had been acquired by few of the settlers who had been in East Africa since 1918. Swahili was the lingua franca of East Africa and was spoken with variable elegance by the members of different tribes. On the whole the best Swahili was spoken by the coastal tribes of Kenya and Tanganyika and, I gathered, by the people of Zanzibar. I should here note that I subsequently discovered that it was of great advantage to pick up a little of the tribal language of one's soldiers. This I did and found that it earned me an easy popularity with the men which could not have been so readily earned in any other way.

Following the course in Swahili I joined 2/4 KAR then stationed at Thika about 20 miles from Nairobi. It was a very happy battalion commanded by a delightful man, Colonel

Rushbrooke, who had been a regular officer in 60th Rifles or the Rifle Brigade before becoming a Kenya farmer in peace time. Within a short time of my joining 2/4 KAR other subalterns and myself were posted as reinforcements to the East African Base Camp in Ceylon. The numbering of battalions in the KAR indicated the territory from which the askari were recruited. The 4th Battalion was the pre-war regular Uganda battalion. When the number of battalions was increased following the outbreak of war, the second numeral in the title of each battalion indicated its origin. Thus 2/4th, 3/4th and 4/4th were all Uganda battalions.

The voyage from Mombasa to Colombo on a British India ship was comfortable and enjoyable. The vessel was designed for tropical waters and we were served by Asian stewards who were incomparably more efficient than the British stewards of the *Cameronia*. We called at the Seychelles but, as we were not allowed ashore, we could only observe their lush beauty from the sea. During the voyage I became particularly well acquainted and friendly with three other subalterns named Brittain, Clarke and Doyle. They were an interesting and varied trio. Eric Brittain, who was the youngest and closest in age to myself, was an outstandingly handsome and charming man. His father was an Anglican parson. Eric was killed shortly after we went into Burma. Trevor Clarke had served in West Africa before joining the KAR. Jimmy Doyle was a Glaswegian who had worked in the Belgian Congo before the war.

South-East Asia Command

On our arrival in Ceylon we went to the East African Base Camp which was situated in a low-lying part of the island and was thickly covered with coconut palms from which coconuts the size of rugby balls regularly thudded on the ground. The atmosphere was humid and depressing. The camp was commanded by an eccentric officer who made himself unpopular with the officers but endeared himself to those of the askari who were Muslims by his knowledge of the Koran. 11th (East African) Division was already in action in Burma and required regular reinforcements. Brittain, Clarke, Doyle and I decided that we would avail ourselves of the first opportunity to go to

Burma, if possible all to the same battalion. Before long we were sailing from Colombo to Calcutta. Thence we proceeded by rail, steamer on the Brahmaputra and trucks to Burma. The only noteworthy feature of this journey, apart from the terror of being driven at high speed along the escarpments of Imphal and Kohima, was a bizarre conversation which I had with a subaltern from an English county regiment, a stranger to me, against whom I was being squeezed in the heat and congestion of the river steamer. Hoping to engage him in friendly conversation, I asked him which battalion he was going to join. This evoked a taciturn 'I'm not'. Undeterred, I asked him what unit he was going to join. 'War Graves Commission' was the reply. I volunteered the comment that this was a cheerful prospect. 'Well,' he replied, 'It's a — sight better than infantry.' I wondered whether I was destined to become one of his clients.

When we reached the Lochchow Gate where the 'road' to the Kabaw Valley began, we were confronted by a Captain Quartermaster who performed the dual function of taking charge of any officer's impedimenta which were not required for fighting and ensuring that no officer proceeded further without an adequate weapon. The only weapon I had was my revolver. I was told that I could keep it if I wanted to but that I would not be allowed to proceed without either a rifle or a sten gun. Conscious of my incompetence as a marksman and the comparative weights of the two weapons, I had no difficulty in selecting the automatic. I knew that the revolver would be useless unless I was locked in a Japanese embrace and left it with the Quartermaster. As a matter of fact, the sten gun was a poorly manufactured and unreliable weapon. I remember Trevor Clarke, enraged by the failure of the spring of his sten gun's magazine, removing the magazine and throwing it after the retreating Japs! Tin hats were also dumped. The headgear of all ranks in the East African Division was the bush hat.

Having satisfied the Quartermaster, we passed on from Tamu down the 'road' to the Kabaw valley to join 4/4 KAR. The monsoon was in progress. The road was, during the dry season, a narrow mud track. During the monsoon it was impassable to wheeled vehicles. Our route led to Kalemyo and thence to Kalewa on the banks of the Chindwin. Heavy equipment such as the barrels and base plates of 3" mortars were carried on the heads of the askari. Parallel to our advance was that of the 5th Indian Division who were proceeding down the Tiddim road to Kalemyo on a mountainous route to our south. On our first night within the area of conflict, remembering what I had been taught as a cadet, I grabbed a pick and shovel and began scratching the ground intending to dig a trench. Within seconds the implements were removed from my grasp by an askari who dug a fully adequate trench in minutes. I never again attempted to dig my own trench.

Shortly after that first night in Burma we reached 4/4 KAR. I was ordered to take over a platoon in 'A' Company commanded by Jack Cooper, a Cambridge man and pre-war colonial servant in Uganda. The second in command of the company was Bobby Carr, the English rugby cap. He was a keep-fit enthusiast but was repeatedly crippled by malaria until, eventually, the medicos gave up and he was sent home. Life in Burma was a mixture of physical exertion and boredom interspersed by short periods of terror. Our progress was laborious, each foot having to be pulled out of the mud. Every evening a 'box' was formed. The box was a defensive perimeter which was formed by battalion, company or platoon, according to which of these units was operating independently. One evening when we were in a platoon box I was chatting to my platoon sergeant in Swahili. He paid me a compliment which I shall never forget. He said that after the war I must settle in Uganda. He would be my head boy and the rest of the platoon would be my house boys. I would thus have thirty odd servants!

The Japs were tireless in patrolling by night, locating our boxes and seeking to induce terror or, at least, sleeplessness in our ranks by the firing of small arms, the exploding of grenades, screaming and the use of our field telephone. The latter purpose was achieved by cutting our lines, attaching their equipment and phoning us to communicate less than endearing messages. 'Me come back to kill you' sticks in the mind. We all slept on scooped out ground at right angles to our trenches so that, if there was an attempted invasion of the box, we could slide forward into a trench on being alerted by a sentry. On the first two occasions that I experienced the Japs' nocturnal fireworks, I stood to all night in my trench, convinced that we were about to be attacked. Thereafter I paid no attention to the fireworks and slept like a log. We never attempted patrolling by night. Even by day map and compass were useless to me in the thick jungle. It was only the extraordinary sense of direction of the older askari which guided me back from patrols to our company and battalion. We were fortunate to be in Burma when the Japs were in retreat after the victories, won at great price, at Imphal and Kohima.

Towards the end of our tour in Burma we had a long and arduous day. We were the leading company of the leading battalion of the brigade. At dawn we had porridge, much fortified by whisky when Jack Cooper produced a bottle for his officers from nowhere. This nourishment was to last us for the day. When we reached what was thought to be journey's end after minor brushes with the Japs, Len Cloete, one of my fellow subalterns, who was as brave as a lion, was shot, apparently in the lower part of the body. Blood and water poured from him. He was convinced that he was about to expire from an abdominal wound which had penetrated his bladder. Happily all that he had suffered was a shot through the bottom which had punctured his water bottle. After Len's wound and when we were about to form a box for the night, we were fired on from a hill to the East. As I was the nearest officer to him at the time, the CO, Ski Galletly of the South Wales Borderers, ordered me to go and take the hill. In the meantime the gunner FOO (Forward Observation Officer) Major Tony English, RA, who was constantly with us and had the only wireless set that worked, ordered the guns of his battery to shell the hill which I was to take.

As I led my weary platoon off on our unwelcome mission I passed Major W M (Mustard) Campbell, Skerrington's grandson, who was in command of one of the other rifle companies of 4/4 KAR. He was tapping a cigarette on his silver cigarette case as though waiting to be served with a drink. Campbell was a legendary character in the KAR with whom he had served since before the war. He won the hearts of all ranks, regardless of colour, by his exceptional bravery which he concealed beneath a cloak of casual indifference. When he saw me with my platoon on that Burmese evening he said 'David, where are you going?' 'I've got to take that bloody hill,' I replied. 'I'll come with you,' he said. This was, of course, far beyond the call of duty since he commanded another company but heartened a dispirited, not to say terrified, subaltern. Thus was I accompanied to our objective. Happily Tony English's guns had done their work so effectively that there was no opposition.

Thenceforward life proceeded more or less uneventfully until we reached the banks of the mighty Chindwin. We made the crossing in small boats by night. Fortunately there was no opposition and we were able to establish a bridgehead on the Eastern bank without casualties. By now it was December. The monsoon had ended and we were relieved by the British 2nd Division. Their soldiers seemed very puny compared with our African askari. Unfortunately they declined to dig trenches until they had sustained unnecessary casualties. We re-crossed the Chindwin, this time by a Bailey bridge which had been constructed by the sappers with remarkable speed. We then went back to Kalemyo where there was now an airfield from which we were flown out to Assam. On our flight out of Burma we saw, almost with disbelief, the miracle which the Corps sappers had worked in transforming the track through the Kabaw Valley into a modern highway. Although we were far from imagining it to be the case at the time, this was effectively the end of our war.

While we were in India resting and re-training in preparation for an expected return to Burma we celebrated VE Day followed, unexpectedly soon, by VJ Day. The latter had, of course, been advanced by the horrific bomb. It did not occur to me at the time nor, as far as I know, to any of my brother officers that the morality of the use of the bomb could be open to question. There was no doubt that the Japanese were the aggressors nor that they had caused enormous casualties and inflicted terrible cruelties. The bomb certainly shortened the war and saved an incalculable number of allied casualties.

One of the lasting friendships I made in the KAR was that of Tony Lunnan. He was in the 3/6 KAR with whom we were brigaded. He was very amiable and of striking character and appearance with unforgettable blue eyes. I first met him after the war in 1974 at the marriage of my half-brother Francis to his sister Rita whom he gave away. I there met Tony's charming wife for the first time. Since then we have all kept in touch.

Before closing my recollections of Burma I must acknowledge the debt which the Division owed to the mobile surgical team which was attached to it. This team consisted of a surgeon, an anaesthetist and a few African medical orderlies. In the jungle they performed their highly skilled work under the most unpropitious conditions. When one of my men was badly shot through the groin while we were attacking the Japs from their rear, I was convinced that the wound would prove mortal. However, he not only survived being carried by stretcher back to our lines but was so successfully treated by the surgeon and his staff that in a short time he made a full recovery. Unfortunately the Divisional Commander, Major-General 'Fluffy' Fowkes, did not appreciate that there were limits to what could be achieved by surgical skill even of the highest quality. This led to what was, strictly speaking, a mutiny. He ordered the mobile surgical team to go out with a fighting patrol. This order the surgeon refused to obey. News of the mutiny was sent by signal to 14th Army HQ and laid before General Slim. Slim sent for his senior medical officer, Brigadier John Bruce, who asked him what he thought. Bruce was himself a distinguished surgeon who subsequently became Regius Professor of Surgery at Edinburgh University and President of the Royal College of Surgeons of Edinburgh. He told Slim that the Divisional Commander was a bloody fool and that the surgeon had acted correctly in disobeying his order. Slim then told Bruce to go to the Divisional HQ and sort the matter out, which he did. This incident was recounted to me long after the war by Sir John Bruce when we were sitting as colleagues on a Medical Appeal Tribunal of which I was the chairman.

I must also record the selfless and fearless devotion of our chaplains. The senior chaplain at 11th East African Division HQ was a charming French Canadian White Father, Father Chiasson, who had been a missionary in East Africa before the war. The chaplain most closely associated with our brigade was a Mill Hill Missionary, Father Farrell. For some reason which I have never understood he violently refused to acquiesce in a recommendation that he be awarded a Military Cross.

Homeward Bound

Once the war was over military life became pointless, but the askari had to be taken back to East Africa and I had to await my turn to go home for demobilisation. Eventually I returned to Kenya with a shipload of askari. Thereafter I marked time in and around Nairobi and Mombasa until my number came up to go home for demobilisation. In Mombasa I met Josephine Devlin who was then a nursing sister in the Colonial Service. We became engaged to be married. My posting home for demobilisation arrived and I flew, without delay, to Cairo. There was then a long pause while I waited, first at Port Said and then at Alexandria, for a westward bound ship. Eventually I sailed from Alex to Toulon and proceeded thence by a very uncomfortable troop train to Calais. I crossed to Dover and went up to London. It was now October, 1946. The weather was unusually severe and I discovered for the first time what life was like in the British Isles when food, drink and fuel were in short supply. After going through the demobilisation procedure, I returned to my mother's house and Edinburgh University.

III   *The Post-War Student (1946-1948)*

Cedant arma togae, concedat laurea laudi
Let arms give place to the toga, laurels to paeans
Cicero: *De Officiis I*

Tendebantque manus ripae ulterioris amore
They stretched forth their hands in longing for the further shore
Virgil: *Aeneid* Book VI

Having been demobilised, and being engaged to be married, I was anxious only to complete my academic and practical training for the bar and to start earning my living as soon as possible. In 1947 Josephine came home and left the Colonial Nursing Service. Her home was in County Tyrone. I visited her there and met her father, who was a widower, and her brothers. She came to stay in my mother's house.

In the summer of 1947 I graduated MA. Thereafter, while nominally attending law lectures at Edinburgh University, I was gaining practical experience with the premier firm of Glasgow solicitors, Maclay Murray & Spens. As I was hoping to be called to the bar in 1948, I could not accept any remuneration from them and existed on my post-war gratuity and ex-serviceman's student grant. In those days a candidate for the bar could not be admitted unless a year had elapsed since he last received remuneration from solicitors. I had been advised, very shrewdly, by Innes Wedderburn to gain experience with Glasgow solicitors before devilling and he had introduced me to Ralph Risk, a partner in Maclay Murray & Spens and subsequently President of the Law Society of Scotland, who agreed to take me on.

I stayed in lodgings in Glasgow and worked hard, by day in the office at 169 West George Street, Glasgow, and by night reading for the Edinburgh LL.B. examinations. While I was with Maclay Murray & Spens I was joined by Tom and John Risk, sons of Ralph, and by Charles Jauncey. They all came as indentured apprentice solicitors. Tom Risk became Governor of the Bank of Scotland and received a knighthood. John Risk became the Secretary of J & P Coats (subsequently Coats, Patons). Charles Jauncey, who was an invalided sailor and a son of the gallant Captain J.H. Jauncey, D.S.O., R.N. of the Russian Convoy, had been at Christ Church. Charles and I soon became close friends. He intended to become a Glasgow solicitor but I suggested to him that he would be happier at the bar. He agreed saying that he would come to the bar if he could succeed in begging or borrowing the necessary funds. He did so and was called to the bar a year after myself. When he was elevated to the House of Lords as a Lord of Appeal in Ordinary he wrote me a kind letter recalling our conversation in Glasgow. While in Glasgow I joined the Glasgow Juridical Society which met for debates once a week except during the Summer.

In the summer session of 1948 I began devilling for Jeffrey Cunningham who was then one of the busiest juniors at the bar. He was not a great orator but was a first class draftsman, precise, concise and accurate, who taught me the essentials of a junior's work and, during the year that I spent with him, took every opportunity to introduce me to his instructing solicitors. In July, 1948 I was called to the bar. This involved the payment in round figures of £500 in respect of Faculty and Widows' Fund dues and Stamp Duty. The current equivalent would be £5,000. In technical terms I was admitted to the Faculty of Advocates or, as used to be said, 'Passed advocate'. J S C Reid, K.C., M.P., subsequently Lord Reid of Drem, was the Dean of Faculty and was the first to welcome me to the bar. I continued to devil until the statutory year of devilling expired. Fortunately, briefs soon began to arrive. I had made it clear to Gilbert McWhannell, my clerk, that I was under the necessity of earning my living without delay and that I was available to any solicitor seeking the services of counsel for 365 days a year.

In 1948 the Labour Government which was the product of the 1945 General Election was in the middle of its term of office. George Thomson, K.C., M.P. was appointed Lord Advocate but there was no 'socialist' counsel at the Scots Bar of sufficient seniority to be appointed Solicitor General. The vacancy was filled by the appointment of D.P. Blades, K.C., a Liberal who was considered to be sufficiently left-inclined to be acceptable. Blades' service was soon rewarded by his elevation to the Bench where he failed to conceal his lack of judicial qualities. When George Emslie tendered a Note of Exception to Blades' charge to a civil jury, his Lordship's reaction was 'I'll sign it and much good may it do you'. Blades was an ignorant bully. At a Glasgow Circuit, where Douglas Reith and I were prosecuting, he attacked Douglas remorselessly because he was impugning the integrity of the police by prosecuting two constables for attempting to pervert the course of justice.

In the Crown Office, H.W. Guthrie, K.C., was Home Advocate Depute before becoming Sheriff of Ayr and Bute for a short time. He was elevated to the bench of the Court of Session at the age of about 45, being preferred to a number of brilliant and much more experienced counsel, presumably because he was a Liberal. As a result, although he was a good lawyer, he was nervous and inflexible and created needless difficulties. He had a pharisaic veneration for the Rules of Court. His interlocutory work was thus an instrument of torture for many junior counsel.

IV   *Stuff Gown (1948-1959)*

Until the post-war era it was unusual for more than two or three to be called to the Scots bar simultaneously. After the war there was a backlog which inflated the numbers. Since then membership of the bar has increased to a size never known before, a by-product of legal aid, the very large increase in the numbers studying law at the universities and the substantial reduction in real terms of the cost of admission to the Faculty of Advocates.

I was one of seven intrants. Of the others Jubb, who never practised, worked for British Aluminium. Douglas Rawson practised in Kuala Lumpur. Bill Hook was and remains a close friend. Bill Hook became a Sheriff at Greenock before moving to Linlithgow and Edinburgh. He had the lease of Wester Kames Castle on Bute where he and Margo provided generous hospitality in the handsome and beautifully situated castle. James Fiddes, a Snell Exhibitioner of Balliol and accomplished pianist, became a sheriff at Hamilton. Bob Inglis, an ebullient personality and first class golfer served as a sheriff at Dundee, Fort William and Paisley. George Emslie became Dean of Faculty before being elevated to the bench. After only about a year in the Outer House George succeeded Hamish Clyde as Lord President and Lord Justice-General. Neil Macvicar should have been called with us but was too preoccupied in pursuing his courtship of the beautiful and charming Marily to spare the time. He displayed a proper sense of priorities and continued to do so throughout his career at the bar. As a result he failed to realise his full potentialities. In his retirement, however, he has put all readers of his autobiographical *A Heart's Odyssey* in his debt with his sensitive record of his love affair with Marily and Corfu. We might fairly have been described as a motley crew.

On the evening of our call Bill and Margo Hook threw a party for us in their flat in Castle Terrace. I assisted Bill in carrying buckets of ale from the Castle Bar, now a superior restaurant, to his flat. It was at the top of a very high staircase and looked out on the southern end of Edinburgh Castle.

On 5 August, 1948 Josephine and I were married at St

Wedding Day, 5 August 1948. L–R: Vera Russell (bridesmaid), the author and Josephine, Willie Brand (best man)

Peter's, Falcon Avenue, Edinburgh. Hugh Gordon officiated. My brother Willie was the best man and Vera Russell was the bridesmaid.

For the next two years our home was in the top flat in Brandon Street which I had bought for £850 with the aid of a loan of £600. Our eldest daughter, Jane, was born on 20 May, 1949. Thereafter we moved to 38 Moray Place which was to be my home and chambers until after my appointment as Solicitor-General in 1970. Madeleine, Lulu and Cecilia were all born when our home was in Moray Place.

From the moment of my admission to the Faculty I was conscious not merely of its corporate spirit but also of the eminent friendliness and helpfulness of my brethren of the bar. During session the Parliament House was a hive of activity. On any court day all practising members of the bar, other than those engaged on criminal circuits, were present, wigged and robed. Between 10 and 10.30 am the advocate's clerks had a hectic time directing their counsel to the appropriate courts and, where there was a conflict of engagements, finding substitutes. In those days when few young juniors had adequate personal libraries it was the common practice to go to the Juridical Library in Charlotte Square in the evenings where one could work all night. The great advantage of that institution was the availability, not only of books but also of the willing advice of juniors more experienced than oneself in problems of drafting pleadings and writing opinions.

Virtually every advocate lived in the New Town. Consequently, the brotherhood of the bar embraced not only its members but also their wives and children. The caretaker of the Juridical Library was Mrs Windebank, a dear old widow who lived in the top floor above the library. She mothered the young bachelors who regularly worked in the library and provided them with tea and cakes. With the extension of library and consulting facilities in the Parliament House, the need for the bar to live in the New Town and to have a library there ceased to exist and the Juridical Library was disposed of.

In the Parliament House it was an education to enjoy the conversation and reminiscences of one's elders and betters in the Coffee Room and the Gown Room. Pre-eminent among these was Arthur Alison, K.C. He had been called to the bar in,

I think, 1896, having been head boy of Rugby. He had achieved a double first in Mods and Greats at Oxford. Alison was a most charming, interesting and self-effacing man. He recalled meeting Robert Louis Stevenson when RLS visited his father's house. Alison spoke in a quiet staccato voice which strangely concentrated one's attention on what he said. He devoted his life to law reporting and editing *Session Cases*. This meant that he never earned more than about £700 pa. He told me that he would have liked to have had a practice but he had only one client – 'An unsatisfactory fellow, sodomy or something of that sort'!

Alison had vivid recollections of the Second Division when it was presided over by Lord Justice-Clerk Macdonald (known as 'Jumbo') sitting with the incongruous and incompatible Lords Young, Moncreiff (a nobleman) and Trayner. It was said that Young, having been Lord Advocate, was aggrieved at never being promoted beyond the rank of Lord Ordinary. He did not conceal his contempt for his brethren, particularly Trayner, and behaved as though he were in the chair. Young had a biting tongue which, like Braxfield in an earlier age, he enjoyed using. On being introduced to Alfred Austin, the Poet Laureate, Young is reputed to have asked him whether he made poetry pay. 'I manage to keep the wolf from the door,' replied Austin. 'Do you read it your poems?' asked Young. Young may have been familiar with the lines attributed to Austin on the illness of the Prince of Wales, afterwards Edward VII: 'Across the wires the electric message came: "He is no better, he is much the same".' Regrettably, it has to be said that Austin was an old Stonyhurst boy; but his obituarist in the Stonyhurst magazine of 1913 made some amends, not by damning him with faint praise, but by refraining from any praise.

When the Second Division was hearing a case of breach of warranty relating to a horse which allegedly 'jibbed', their Lordships exchanged the following observations. Lord Trayner: 'The horse must have been an ass.' The Lord Justice-Clerk: 'An ass doesn't jib.' Lord Young: 'Your Lordship should know.' When sitting in the Outer House Lord Young heard a motion to appoint a member of the bar as a commissioner to take the evidence of a witness in Paisley, who was unfit to travel to Edinburgh. 'I'll appoint MacRobert,' replied his Lordship, 'he knows the language.' MacRobert was the son of a well-known solicitor in Paisley a town whose inhabitants had their own patois. In the Second Division, when Young became bored, he told the Lord Justice-Clerk, 'We've had enough of this for today.' If the Lord Justice-Clerk declined to adjourn, Young spent the remainder of the sitting tearing his papers into small pieces. On one occasion when Young and Trayner were walking down the Mound together Trayner referred to the fact that his portrait was hanging in the RSA Exhibition and persuaded Young to come into the Academy to see it. Having been led to the painting Young stood in front of it in silence. Eventually Trayner asked him whether he thought the picture was like him. 'Painfully' was Young's reply.

Another elder statesman when I was called to the bar was Professor Candlish Henderson, K.C., who was the joint author of an invaluable textbook – Gloag and Henderson's *Introduction to the Law of Scotland*. He was also the author of *Henderson on Vesting,* commonly treated with the respect normally accorded only to the institutional writers, Stair, Erskine and Bell, and Hume on Crime. I sat at the feet of Candlish Henderson during the last year of his tenure of the chair of Scots Law at Edinburgh University. He was the last holder of that chair who was not barred by the terms of his appointment from private practice. Candlish had high standards which his students had to satisfy before they could graduate. When I got to know him as a brother of the bar I found him dry but entertaining. He had a small but esoteric practice which was restricted to black letter law, trusts, conveyancing and land ownership. He respected judges who had 'subtle' minds but can have had little experience of criminal work or run-of-the-mill claims for damages.

Within a few months of my call to the bar Reid, the Dean of Faculty, was elevated to the House of Lords as a Lord of Appeal in Ordinary. His was the last such appointment directly from the Scots bar without any intervening judicial experience. His predecessor, Lord Thankerton, had in 1935 provoked Lord Dunedin to complain to the Lord Chancellor that he was 'making himself a veritable nuisance by excessive talking'. (See *Judges* by David Pannick, p. 84.) It was said that Reid was elevated because, as an Opposition Front Bench spokesman, he was a serious thorn in the Labour Government's flesh. Be that as it may, it was generally agreed by the bar that his appointment was entirely appropriate. During the long years that he sat in the Judicial Committee of the House of Lords, mostly in the chair, he distinguished himself as probably the most outstanding Scots lawyer to hold that office. He was also highly respected by the English bench and bar. I take pride in the fact that I instigated the commissioning by the Faculty of the painting of Reid's portrait.

Reid had succeeded Ronald Morison as Dean of Faculty, the latter having had to resign on account of matrimonial problems. Ronald's father, T.B. Morison, had been a judge and his son Malcolm is a judge. Ronald was undoubtedly the most accomplished master of advocacy of his day. Jim Shaw, subsequently Lord Kilbrandon, told me that in his opinion Ronald was in the late 1940s and until he gave up practice probably the pre-eminent advocate, not only at the Scots bar, but in the United Kingdom. This was high and reliable praise indeed as Jim had had direct experience of Ronald and of Cyril Radcliffe, Q.C., then the most distinguished counsel at the English bar, appearing against each other in the House of Lords.

In my opinion, Jim who was himself elected Dean of Faculty in 1957, had a better brain than Ronald but the latter was the more dedicated advocate. Although I was only a tyro when Ronald was at the height of his fame, he was always very kind to me and never failed to write to me at each stage of my career long after he had left the bar. He was short and physically insignificant but electrified the atmosphere of any court that he was addressing. He had a beautiful voice which lent additional force to his elegant language. Ronald was both a brilliant orator and an highly skilled cross-examiner. He achieved his results by making the best use of his natural gifts and by applying himself with meticulous thoroughness and industry to the preparation of every case which he undertook. He told me that he was never interested in the law as such. His interest was advocacy. He mastered enough law for each case as it turned up.

At about the same time as Reid went to the House of Lords Fred Strachan, K.C, who was Vice-Dean, was appointed to the bench of the Court of Session. Fred Strachan had been defeated in the election for Dean by Ronald Morison. There was thus a brief interregnum when the Faculty had neither Dean nor Vice-Dean. In the event, Jock Cameron was elected Dean, *nem con.* James Walker was elected Vice-Dean after a contest with Bill Milligan who subsequently became Solicitor-General and then Lord Advocate and a judge. For some years before becoming a judge, Fred Strachan had been the most distinguished lawyer at the senior bar. Like Raymond Asquith at the English bar, his reputation was based on the reliability of his advice rather than on his powers of advocacy. Strachan was an outstandingly good judge. His extreme taciturnity could, however, be unnerving to counsel. It was as remarkable as his patience which was maintained despite the pain resulting from the loss of a leg in the 1914-1918 war.

A year or two after Jock had been elected Dean I was instructed to accompany him to Shetland as his junior to appear before Randall Philip, Q.C., known as 'The Puffin' on account of his physical resemblance to that bird. Randall had been appointed to hold a public inquiry into a wool-marketing scheme. It was an interesting experience, particularly as I had never previously been to Shetland. There were objectors to the proposed scheme and the inquiry lasted for about a week. The economy of Shetland in those days rested solely on wool and fish. There was no oil industry. The women of the island knitted as naturally as they breathed, knitting while they walked. On our last night in Shetland we had a mini bar dinner organised by Robbie Wallace, the local sheriff. Philip ultimately reported to the Secretary of State in favour of the scheme. The Shetlanders then held a public meeting at which it was decided not to proceed with the scheme which they had successfully promoted! Randall received a knighthood as Procurator to the Church of Scotland. He was probably the last of the practising gentlemen silks who never went on the Bench.

In 1950 the Faculty marked the centenary of Robert Louis Stevenson's birth by holding a splendid dinner in the Parliament Hall. The Dean of Faculty (Cameron) presided but, apart from him, there was no precedence in the seating arrangements. From the Lord President to the most junior member of the bar we all dined as equals. This caused Lord Gibson, the Chairman of the Land Court, to absent himself from the dinner. When Gibson had received notice of the dinner from George Walker, the

Treasurer of the Faculty, he sent a cheque for the appropriate amount to Walker with a covering letter in which he said that he expected to be given appropriate precedence at the dinner. Walker replied that no one would be given any precedence as we were all dining as brethren of the Faculty. Gibson then wrote to Walker saying that, as the condition on which he had agreed to attend the dinner had not been purified, he would not be coming and asked for the return of his cheque!

Gibson was a very eccentric person. He had been a Labour Member of Parliament and, during the war, was the senior Labour member of the Scots bar. As the government was a coalition, he would have had a claim to the Solicitor-Generalship, if that office fell vacant. In order to avoid this eventuality the Lord Advocate (Cooper) persuaded David King Murray who was then Chairman of the Land Court to resign and return to the bar. The chairmanship of the Land Court was then offered to Gibson, who accepted it. Tam Innes, the Lord Lyon, assisted by Charles Jauncey, then devised a Land Court mace for Gibson, constructed, it was said, with a broom handle, a tobacco tin and a lip stick holder. As Chairman of the Land Court Gibson, upon whom Jock Cameron conferred the soubriquet of 'adipocere', was not merely unsound but absurd. For example, he not only accompanied the agricultural members of the court on their inspections of crofts but did so wearing judicial robes! On an appeal from the Land Court to the Court of Session the Lord President (Clyde) observed that Parliament did not make the Land Court a law unto itself.

Like other stupid men, Gibson was pompous and vain. He was thus led into a trap laid by Jock Cameron and James Walker when appearing with their juniors before him. Gibson opened the proceedings by telling them that they should follow the procedure of the Inner House of the Court of Session and have speeches from junior counsel first followed by speeches from their leaders. Cameron replied that, after discussion with his learned friend, it had been agreed that, as befitted the dignity of the Land Court, the appropriate model was the House of Lords! There would thus be one speech only from each side of the Bar delivered by senior counsel. Thus was Gibson's vanity satisfied and the proceedings abbreviated.

On Gibson's appointment to the Land Court, King Murray

was appointed Solicitor-General. In 1945 he was elevated to the Bench with the judicial title of Lord Birnam. He was a charming man who was particularly kind to young juniors. He was also a man of wide experience and common sense which made him an excellent judge of first instance. One felt that his decisions were correct even when they were reversed.

The Stevenson Centenary

The Stevenson dinner was a huge success due largely to the brilliant speech made by the Dean of Faculty in proposing the toast to the memory of Robert Louis Stevenson. Lord Cameron has very kindly provided me with a transcript of that speech which, with his permission, is appended to these anecdotes. At the close of the formal proceedings, Alness, a former Lord Justice-Clerk and a former Secretary of State for Scotland, rose to say 'a few words'. This was entirely in character. He could not let an occasion pass without providing his embellishment. Thus it came to be said that Alness's obituaries and supplementary obituaries provided an additional terror to death.

An Inverness Trial – Lord Mackay

In May 1953 I was instructed by David MacEwan of Henderson & Jackson, W.S., acting as the Edinburgh correspondent of his brother Robin of Stewart Rule & Co., Inverness, to defend one of two men who were accused of raping two Australian hitchhikers on the road to Kyleakin. In those days the normal practice in Inverness was for the circuit judge as well as all the counsel to stay in the Station Hotel. On this occasion, as we all knew, the judge was to be Lord Mackay and he was going to stay at the Station Hotel. There were four counsel. Norman Sloan as the Advocate Depute led for the Crown. He was assisted by Lorn Cowie (now Lord Cowie). Muir Russell defended the first-named accused and I defended the second-named accused. As none of us had any desire to enjoy Mackay's company outside the court, we all stayed at the Caledonian Hotel.

Judging by what one has read about Lord Justice-Clerk Eskgrove, Mackay might have taken him as his model. As

Cockburn wrote in his *Memorials of His Time* (1946 edition, p.84), 'Never once did Eskgrove do or say anything which had the slightest claim to be remembered for any intrinsic merit. The value of all his words and actions consisted in their absurdity.' In addition to being ludicrous, Eskgrove was verbose and self-important. Each of those adjectives applied equally to Mackay. Throughout the many years that he was a member of the Second Division, sitting under a succession of illustrious Lord Justice-Clerks, he reduced that court to a shambles with his constant interruptions. John Wilson's famous parody of a hearing in the Second Division entitled *Higginbottom's Trustees* in which no counsel got beyond saying 'My Lords, in this case I appear', was not far removed from reality. When, after the war, Lord Patrick was chosen to be one of the judges to try Japanese War Criminals, Lord Cooper remarked to T.B. Simpson, K.C., 'It would have served them right to send Mackay – death by a thousand "Buts".' Mackay's loquacity had been notorious since his days at the bar. According to one story, he was in full torrent before the Second Division when the one o'clock gun was heard. Rising with alacrity the Lord Justice-Clerk said, 'Don't let a mere gun stop you, Mr Mackay. We will be back at 2 o'clock.'

My first experience of Mackay as a criminal judge had been on the Glasgow circuit – also in a case of alleged rape. I felt a heavy weight of responsibility as my client, a marine engineer, was a respectable man whose domestic life and career could have been ruined by a conviction. The Crown case was hopeless and ought not to have been insisted in but, with Mackay on the bench, any result was possible. The evidence was in short compass. Both the Advocate Depute (Ian Robertson) and myself addressed the jury quite shortly. Mackay, who was incapable of being concise or precise, then commenced his charge to the jury. He devoted the first chapter of it to deploring the brevity of the speeches of counsel. Happily, the jury had no difficulty in acquitting my client.

Inverness in May 1953, presented an idyllic picture, particularly from the castle which housed the court. The castle, built on a hilltop, overlooks the town on one side and the Ness on the other. In front of the castle stands the statue of Flora Macdonald who befriended Bonnie Prince Charlie. The weather was perfect. As was customary in those days, the local regiment, in this case the Camerons, mounted a guard of honour outside the castle for inspection by the judge every morning. Not to be outshone by the kilts and bonnets of the Camerons, Mackay paraded daily in a silk hat and morning coat. Seldom, if ever, can his Lordship's vanity have been better satisfied. After the usual preliminaries the trial in the case of *Her Majesty's Advocate v McCulloch & Mackay* got under way. The eccentric comings and goings of the bibulous sheriff clerk, Murdo Mackintosh, who had no part to play in the proceedings of the High Court but who insisted an sitting beneath the bench when not seeking refreshment, aroused no particular interest. The capital of the Highlands has its own standards and customs. It was only towards the end of the trial when the sheriff clerk sought to walk between the jury and the Advocate-Depute while the latter was addressing them that any attempt was made to restrain the sheriff clerk's perambulations.

The setting of the case was that my client was driving his car along the road towards Kyle initially with McCulloch sitting in the passenger seat beside him and the two girls sitting on the back seat. After some time the car was stopped and McCulloch and one of the girls exchanged places. There was then some exchange of familiarities between each of the two couples. This culminated in my client leaving the car with the girl who had been sitting beside him. The other couple remained in the back of the car. My client and his companion had sexual intercourse on the grass verge on the road side. According to my client this intercourse took place with the girl's consent. The other accused's defence was that he did not have intercourse with his companion but he admitted that he had indecently assaulted her. As my client's defence to the charge of rape was consent, I put the question of consent in issue as soon as I cross-examined the girl. She, of course, denied that the intercourse was consensual. In due course my client gave evidence along the lines already indicated.

After Russell and I had addressed the jury, Mackay proceeded to direct them. That address was so fantastic that it is worthy of being examined in a little detail, as I shall do later. Suffice it to say that, from a strictly legal point of view, it was only of interest insofar as it contained the clearest possible misdirection on the question of consent. As I have already said, I put the question of consent in issue at the earliest opportunity and kept it there throughout the trial. Mackay told the jury that they might consider it extraordinary that they had never heard a word about consent until my client gave evidence. I have never been able to understand why Sloan, as the Advocate-Depute, did not seek to correct Mackay at the end of his charge. In Scotland the presiding judge does not sum up as in England but charges the jury.

Mackay began his charge to the jury by telling them that he fancied 'no such case ever came before a jury in the course of the world's history'. He also referred to the *locus* as one of General Wade's roads, an assertion that was contradicted by the Lord Justice-General in the appeal court! In the course of his charge to the jury Mackay said, in relation to my client, that the only defence 'now' was consent. 'The case as I see it has entirely changed its aspect since the two men went into the witness box for themselves.' After referring to the admittedly consensual love-making between the two couples, his Lordship went on,

'But, ladies and gentlemen, it is still as much [the law] as it was in the time of Hume and Alison 120 years ago, it is the duty of the male to refrain from invading the female body, however far these matters nowadays may go. It occurred to me once I had read the old passage, to tell you that those passages are all taken from Hume and Alison 120 years ago, and no doubt absolutely described the law of that day. In those days the typical sort of case no doubt was the bold bad baron of Victorian times who assaulted minor servants and the rest, or two rough country persons falling in love with one another and not resisting, that sort of thing. Now I think we must modernise our ideas when we have what indeed we have an instance of here, women going voluntarily on 500 mile tramps, picking up lifts from men in lorries and the rest as they go and so getting help, and risking the consequences, and may I say again, exposing their limbs in very attractive guise, which in the old days would have been covered by petticoats.'

After referring to the fact that, in the course of the journey, the car was stopped to enable the rearrangement of the seating to be effected, his Lordship continued:

'I for my part am quite willing to accept it as clearly proved that the women at that stage were willing enough with all that drink in them, and seeing these strange men to have a little sexual fun together, but are you to consider that by so doing they committed themselves to receiving the male organ if the male organ was presented to them?'

And so the charge meandered on to its end, the transcript extending to 345 pages of foolscap.

The jury found McCulloch guilty of ravishing the girl who was beside him in the back of the car. They also convicted my client, Mackay, of ravishing the girl with whom he had had intercourse on the grass verge and of being guilty art and part in McCulloch's rape of the other girl on the basis that he had given McCulloch verbal encouragement. I immediately told Robin MacEwen that, in my opinion, our client should appeal on the ground of misdirection of the jury by the judge. The misdirection was plainly of the gravest kind as it cast serious doubt on the credibility of my client.

When instructions for the appeal reached Henderson & Jackson W.S., in Edinburgh, David MacEwen asked me if I would like to be led in the appeal by the Dean of Faculty (Cameron, Q.C.). I was naturally delighted by this suggestion. I was confident that the Dean would achieve a total quashing of my client's convictions on the basis of Mackay's gross misdirection and the generally ludicrous nature of his charge to the jury. Alas! I was over-sanguine. The Lord Justice-General (Cooper) presided at the hearing of the appeal. Cameron was undoubtedly an advocate of distinction and presented the appeal with a speech of great power. Cooper, whose nickname was 'The wee grocer', confined himself to bridling at the Dean's criticism of the trial judge. Cooper's soubriquet was not a reflection on his intellect, which was massive, but was prompted by his stature, his appearance when not on the Bench and his occasional lack of judicial bearing when on the Bench.

The extraordinary result of the appeal was that our client's conviction of being art and part in McCulloch's rape was upheld but his conviction of raping the woman with whom he had admittedly had intercourse was quashed. It is difficult to regard the result as other than illogical as the trial judge's ill-founded aspersions on Mackay's credibility necessarily affected his convictions in relation to both women. Mackay's sentence was reduced from seven years to five years. McCulloch, who had also appealed, had his sentence reduced from six years to five years.

Lord President Cooper and the Inner House

The First Division of the Court of Session during the years when Cooper presided as Lord President was an intellectually bracing court in which to appear as counsel. The other judges who sat in that Division were Carmont, Russell and Keith. Cooper had a considerable respect for Carmont's ability which he did not have for the other members of the court. James Keith, who became a Lord of Appeal in Ordinary with the title of Lord Keith of Avonholm, had an independent and original mind of high quality. He was known as Thrawn Jimmy. If, in the course of a hearing Cooper apprehended that Carmont was taking a different view of the case being heard to that of himself, he would pause in his tracks but he was indifferent to whether Lord Russell or Lord Keith disagreed with him. He knew that, in any event, Russell would eventually concur in his opinion albeit after a lengthy paraphrase of it. On a celebrated occasion when a case which had been taken to avizandum, that is to say where the judges had taken time to consider their opinions, was being advised in the First Division, Cooper as Lord President delivered the leading opinion. Lord Carmont's opinion consisted of a concurrence in which he said, 'I agree with the opinion of your Lordship in the chair and there is nothing useful which I can add.' Lord Russell in giving his opinion said, 'I also agree with the opinion of your Lordship in the chair and further I agree with the additional words which have fallen from the lips of my brother Lord Carmont.' These remarks are not intended to belittle Albert Russell's character and ability as a judge. He had an instinctive understanding which enabled him to preside with total command and serenity over any criminal trial. On or off the bench he was always charming.

There were occasions in the First Division when Cooper was presiding over the hearing of an appeal or reclaiming motion when he would lead his brethren to run violently with the argument of one side before the hearing was completed. On one

Stuff Gown (1948-1959)   43

such occasion when Hill Watson was the senior counsel for the respondent, he began his speech by saying that he gathered from what had fallen from their Lordships that nothing he could say would affect their minds. That observation, although quite improper, had certainly been provoked by the behaviour of the Bench. The interesting sequel was that Carmont, and not the Lord President, pounced on Hill Watson, who promptly acknowledged the impropriety of what he had said. Cooper's lack of command in such a situation was probably due to the fact that for practically all his life he was dominated by his mother.

Before leaving my recollections of Tommy Cooper I should mention an episode in the Advocates Library during his tenure of the office of Lord President and Lord Justice-General. There was at that time a well-known and accomplished comedian who was called Tommy Cooper. His hallmark was a fez which he invariably wore on the stage. When the comedian visited one of the Edinburgh theatres large posters were displayed showing his quizzically humorous face topped by a fez. Accompanying his portrait was a list of his skills. These included 'Precognitions'. What precognitions are in the world of the theatre I know not but, for the lawyer, they are statements given to solicitors of what witnesses are expected to say if called upon to give evidence. On the occasion of the comedian's visit to Edinburgh a member of the bar obtained one of the posters and displayed it in the Advocates Library. It was, naturally, a source of considerable amusement!

Cooper belonged to the generation which suffered the worst casualties in the 1914-18 war. Many of his contemporaries at the bar not only went to the war but earned awards for gallantry and suffered grave and, in some cases, fatal injuries. According to the biographical preface to his *Selected Papers*, Cooper was rejected for military service on medical grounds. Be that as it may, his failure to enlist earned him the derision of those of his contemporaries who fought and survived. Apart from Lord Cameron, they are now all gone but, during my early years at the bar, they used to lunch together annually in the Cafe Royal after the Anniversary Meeting of the Faculty. On these occasions they drank toasts, first, to the memory of their brethren who went to the war but did not return and, secondly, to those who never went coupled with the name of Tommy Cooper.

Cooper's tenure of the office of Lord President coincided almost exactly with that of George Thomson as Lord Justice-Clerk. Thomson was a great judge whose ability has not yet been fully recognised.

The Infuriated Cow

Shortly after the Inverness rape trial I appeared in the Inverness Sheriff Court, again instructed by Robin MacEwan, to appear for Hamilton's Auction Marts Ltd to resist a claim for damages in respect of the destruction caused by a cow which had escaped from the Inverness Market. The case *(Cameron v Hamilton's Auction Marts Ltd and Another 1955 S.L.T. (Sh. Ct.) 74)* has the distinction of being included in Megarry's *Miscellany-at-Law* as the case of the infuriated cow. Having escaped from the mart, the cow climbed a stairway over a shop, fell through the upper floor, and in her struggles turned on a tap, so flooding the shop. The second defender was the farmer who had sent the cow to be sold in the market. I persuaded the sheriff-substitute (Grant, commonly known as 'Rothiemerchus' because he was the laird of Rothiemerchus) to sustain a preliminary plea *(anglice demurrer)* to hold that the claim was unfounded in law and could not succeed and to dismiss the action. Grant sustained my plea and dismissed the action so far as laid against the first defenders. Grant's judgement was unsuccessfully appealed to the sheriff principal (McKechnie, Q.C.) who found himself 'forced to the conclusion that a gate-crashing, stair climbing, floor bursting, tap-turning cow is something *sui generis,* for whose depredations the law affords no remedy unless there was foreknowledge of some such propensities.'

Some Sheriff Court Cases

Most of my time was devoted to civil work in the Court of Session but civil cases in the sheriff courts, particularly in Glasgow, provided a useful source of work. The Glasgow Sheriff Court was then situated in Ingram Street. Its external design escaped one's attention as it was inconspicuous, consisting of wholly blackened stone. Its interior was a maze of corridors giving access to numerous courtrooms as well as to the offices of the procurator fiscal and his deputes and to the sheriff clerk and his deputes. It was only after years of trial and error that the novice in this temple of justice could, without deviation, immediately attain his goal.

The interior decoration and facilities provided for members of the legal profession were remarkable and, one trusts, unique. The decor could only be described as 'Victorian lavatorial', the walls being lined with glazed green tiles. Unhappily, the impression of ample sanitation was belied by the facts. Any member of the legal profession who required to answer the call of nature had to obtain a key from the gentleman in the library – who rejoiced in the grandiloquent title of 'Librarian' – in order to obtain access to what Americans call the 'Rest Room'. The functions of the Librarian were of a custodial rather than literary nature. He did not expect to be asked for the key to the lavatory but for the key to the 'Toilet' or simply 'the key'. He handed it over with the admonition, 'Mind tae bring it back.' What sanitary provision was made for the needs of the public I do not know. It can only have been Dickensian. As the Ingram Street building has now been replaced by a modern court house on the south of the Clyde, the atmosphere of the old Sheriff Court will linger only in the memories of a diminishing number of lawyers and their clients.

I was also fortunate in being employed in country sheriff courts such as Duns, where the eccentric C de B Murray presided, and Oban and Dunoon by solicitors who did not practise advocacy and instructed me whenever their clients were involved in litigation in their local sheriff courts. Murray had been the sheriff-substitute in Stornoway before being appointed to Duns but, throughout, his home was in Moray Place in Edinburgh. When T.B. Simpson told some of his brethren that Murray had an intelligent son, his explanation of how he had acquired this information was that he had heard the boy tell his father that he was a bloody fool.

Sheriff Court work was generally less onerous than that of the High Court and the Court of Session and was often humorous. In one such case I defended a bus driver in Dunoon who had been charged with being drunk in charge of his bus, contrary to section 15 of the Road Traffic Act 1930. He and a colleague had been employed to convey in their buses the

Clydebank Unionist Association (Ladies' section) on their annual outing. Having ventured as far north as Oban and inspected a shinty match, the party commenced their return journey. When they reached Inverary the ladies, being tortured by thirst, persuaded the drivers to stop their buses. Having disembarked, they concussed the unwilling drivers into accompanying them to a hostelry. There they remained until closing time. During this period the drivers had each reluctantly consumed one glass of lager.

On leaving the inn the party was followed back to the parked buses by the local gendarmerie. When all were safely aboard and the engines had been started the officers of the law invited the drivers to accompany them to the police station, which they did. As those were the simple pre-breathalyser days, the police had then to find and persuade a doctor to come to the police station. A doctor eventually arrived and examined the drivers. He pronounced one to be sober and the other so intoxicated as to be unfit to have proper control of his vehicle. The latter was duly charged with a contravention of section 15.

The matter culminated in a summary trial before Sheriff Douglas Donald in Dunoon. The procurator fiscal adduced the evidence of the police and the doctor. I had, however, several witnesses to lead for the defence as my instructing solicitor had cited a large proportion of the Clydebank Unionist ladies to come to Dunoon for the trial. Each of these deponed that the accused had consumed unwillingly and at their insistence a single glass of lager. At the end of the day Sheriff Donald delivered a judgment of Solomon in which, while acquitting the accused, he commended the police for the correct and proper zeal which they had displayed.

Civil Juries

During the 1950s and 1960s there was a large volume of reparation work in the Court of Session. This consisted mostly of actions of damages for personal injuries arising out of industrial accidents and road accidents. The majority of them were tried by juries. The National Coal Board, Clyde stevedoring companies and steel companies were constantly being sued by their employees. The British Transport Commission as operator of the railway was also a popular target. The Shipping Federation covered the claims against the shipping and stevedoring companies. The Iron & Steel Federation covered the steel companies but Colvilles Ltd retained control of the actions in which they were involved. As a junior I acted for several of the stevedoring companies, generally led by Hector McKechnie, Q.C. I also acted for Colvilles Ltd with Manuel Kissen, Q.C., as my senior.

At that time there was a vogue for injured workmen to claim that they had suffered psychological traumata in addition to physical injuries. In support of these claims psychiatrists, some of whom became familiar figures in the courts, were called to give evidence. One of these was always referred to as Professor— although he held no chair. McKechnie, who had an uncontrollable sense of humour, in addressing the jury after the 'Professor' had given evidence in support of a docker's claim said, 'Ladies and gentlemen, those of us who are familiar with these courts know that Professor— is simply the Sir Roderick Glossop of the law courts.' There was no apparent reaction from the jurors due, no doubt, to ignorance of the works of P G. Wodehouse. Be that as it may, it is rash for counsel to make jokes in the presence of jurors or, to go to the sublime, when addressing the Judicial Committee of the House of Lords.

McKechnie's real forte as a counsel was in the abstruse realms of conveyancing and heraldry. In these subjects he had an intellectual ascendancy which was appreciated in the First Division when Cooper was Lord President. If the chair of Scots Law at Edinburgh University had not been made full-time, McKechnie would have been an ideal candidate for it. Unfortunately, he thought he would glide onto the Bench and, when he found that this was not to be, he became demoralised.

Advocate-Depute

In 1956 I was appointed an Advocate-Depute, that is to say a prosecuting counsel who has been commissioned by the Lord Advocate, and thereafter I regularly prosecuted cases in the High Court and, in the Crown Office, marked papers sent in by procurators fiscal for prosecution or otherwise. But before my appointment to the Crown Office, I gained some experience of prosecuting from 1954 onwards as Sheriff Court Advocate-

Depute and as Extra Advocate-Depute for the Glasgow Circuit.

In the Hawick Sheriff Court I prosecuted a dentist before the sheriff principal (Ross McLean, Q.C.) and a jury for indecent assault on some of his male patients. He was defended by Jock Cameron. There was no substantial defence on the merits. After the jury had returned a verdict of guilty, Cameron led a doctor on the staff of a mental hospital, who said that he was willing to receive the dentist as a patient. In cross-examination my single question to the doctor was whether he professed to cure moral defects. He replied in the negative. Ross McLean pronounced a sentence of imprisonment. I doubt whether such a sentence for that type of conduct would nowadays be considered appropriate unless the accused had a relevant criminal record, which was absent in this case, or his victims were minors. It would, at least, be subject to criticism. In my opinion, the best reason for not sending such a person to prison is that he would be likely to corrupt other prisoners or, alternatively, be subjected to violence at their hands.

The Homicide Act 1957 introduced the novel concept of capital and non-capital murder. Until the passing of that Act all convictions for murder in Scotland attracted the death sentence. In practice that sentence had, since at least 1930, seldom been carried out. The accused was almost invariably reprieved and his sentence was commuted to life imprisonment. There is, however, no doubt in my mind that the existence of capital punishment deterred the majority of professional criminals from carrying or using potentially lethal weapons and from associating with the minority who did. Whether or not one is a supporter of capital punishment, the Homicide Act of 1957 must rank as one of the most absurd pieces of legislation of this century and, in view of the standard of much other legislation, that is saying a good deal. The 1957 Act abolished the death penalty for all murder other than murder done in the course or furtherance of theft, murder by shooting or by causing an explosion, murder to prevent or resist lawful arrest or to effect or assist escape from lawful custody, the murder of a police officer or of persons assisting him, the murder of a prison officer or of a person assisting him by a prisoner, and murder committed on more than one occasion. In terms of section 5(3) of the Act capital murder had to be charged as such.

Shortly after the passing of the 1957 Act I prosecuted what, I believe, was the first case of murder in Scotland which was affected by the Act. The accused was charged with non-capital murder in respect that he had murdered in Glasgow a woman and her children 'on one occasion'. At the time of the murders the husband of the murdered woman and father of her children was a prisoner in Barlinnie Prison. Why the accused went to the house where the woman and her children were living and murdered them all, using sauce bottles as weapons, I do not know; but, because it was all done on one occasion it was non-capital murder. If the accused had taken time off for a rest and/or refreshment between one or more of the murders, it would have been murder on more than one occasion and he would have been charged with capital murder. As it was, the accused pled guilty to the non-capital murders with which he was charged and was only concerned, as his counsel told the judge, that he should not be incarcerated in a Scottish prison where his fellow inmates might well inflict on him the punishment which the legislature had prevented the court from imposing. This case demonstrated that the provisions of the 1957 Act were too ridiculous to remain part of the law. In the result Parliament drifted into the total abolition of capital punishment for murder, that punishment being retained solely for treason.

My most stimulating experience as an advocate-depute lay in prosecuting cases before Lord Hill Watson who, unhappily, survived his appointment to the bench only by a few years. Lawrence Hill Watson had a sound and quick mind and a good sense of humour. Although his practice at the bar had consisted mostly of commercial work, he was the ideal judge for dealing with the crude assaults which formed the staple diet on the Glasgow Circuit. It was impossible for counsel to go too fast for Lawrence. Consequently, I was able on occasion to dispose of two trials in one day when prosecuting before him. After the jury for the first case had been empanelled the unempanelled jurors were told to come back at 2 pm for the next case.

In those days the late Frank Duffy appeared for a large proportion of the accused on the Glasgow Circuit. Frank was one of those improbable members of the bar whom everybody loves. Why he came to the bar was and remained a mystery. It was difficult to imagine how he had ever passed any examination but he had an air of innocence which ingratiated him even to the scholarly Lord President Cooper. On one occasion when a morning case before Hill Watson had run into the afternoon, Frank discovered that the unempanelled jurors for the afternoon case had been sitting in the public benches while he had been addressing the jury in the first case. He came to me in great indignation complaining that I ought not to have allowed this to happen. I, non-plussed, asked Frank what was wrong. He replied that what was wrong was that the jurors for the next case had heard his speech before the trial had begun! Frank's civil practice consisted in appearing with Clifford Watt, Q.C. in jury trials when he vociferously tendered unacceptable advice to his senior.

Poor Frank! He went out in a blaze of glory. Shortly after taking silk he had a stroke and collapsed while addressing the jury in a murder trial in Inverness. Fortunately, his junior was the outstandingly able Alastair Horsfall who became a sheriff and then a member of the Lands Tribunal. The trial judge (Sorn) granted an adjournment until the following day and Alastair took up the invidious task of completing the speech to the jury. Frank lived on for a few months after his stroke but was never able to resume practice.

I found the office of advocate-depute most satisfying and in accordance with the best traditions of Scots law and practice. It is misleading to describe our system as adversarial. The duty of prosecuting counsel is not to obtain a conviction but to present the Crown case fully and fairly before the jury. He should not hesitate to abandon a prosecution if it becomes clear that a conviction would not be warranted.

The Thurso Boy

During my time as an advocate-depute the Procurator Fiscal at Wick reported to the Crown Office a complaint against the police alleging that two constables on duty one evening in Thurso had taken a teenage boy up a close where one of them had assaulted him. On the face of the papers it appeared that the constables had been dealing with an unruly and insulting boy and that one of the constables had slapped him, but there was no proof of which of them had done so. I formed the opinion that the public interest would not be served by a prosecution but, as it was the type of case which was liable to have repercussions, I sent the papers to the Solicitor-General (Bill Grant) for confirmation of my opinion. Bill returned the papers expressing his concurrence. I accordingly instructed the Procurator Fiscal that there should be no prosecution.

There the matter would have ended had it not been for the intervention of the local Member of Parliament (Robertson), an independent conservative, egged on by the opposition. At the end of the day the Prime Minister (Macmillan) felt obliged to concede the holding of a public inquiry. The inquiry, held in Inverness under the chairmanship of Lord Sorn with two lay assessors, provided a Roman holiday for the bar, much public entertainment and a boomerang for the slapped boy. Sorn appointed the Dean of Faculty (Jim Shaw, subsequently Lord Kilbrandon) as counsel to the inquiry. He was responsible for adducing all evidence which appeared to him to be relevant. The witnesses described what they saw and heard on the night in question when the youth was alleged to have been assaulted. One of the female witnesses recounted some of the obscene language which she had heard. This led to Jim Shaw asking her in a celebrated 'spoonerism', 'Were you fucked by the word shock?' The inquiry found that the youth, after behaving provocatively, had in fact been assaulted by one or other of the two policemen but that there was no evidence to prove who was guilty of the assault. In my opinion, the whole affair was a great waste of time and money and, like many inquiries, was counterproductive in relation to the interests of those seeking it.

In 1959 I took silk and, as was the practice then, I resigned my office as an advocate-depute. Only the Home, or senior, Advocate-Depute was a member of the senior bar. I took silk with some trepidation, having a wife and four children to support. I was fortunate and never had cause to regret the move. I was kept busy with an entirely civil practice until 1964 when the Lord Advocate, Ian Shearer (subsequently Lord Avonside), invited me to become Home Advocate-Depute. The appointment did not last long as there was soon a change of government and in those days the advocates-depute went out of office with the Lord Advocate.

Of all the judges before whom I prosecuted cases in the High

Court Charles Mackintosh, a charming man, was the most inno-
cent and naive. Despite the fact that he had served as a junior
officer in the Royal Scots throughout the 1914-18 war, he did
not understand much of the earthy language in which the 'lower
orders', never mind the criminals, expressed themselves. He had
had a rarified practice, his experience of criminal work being
restricted to doing his share of defending impecunious criminals. In those pre-legal aid days it was the professional duty of
senior counsel to defend those accused of murder when asked to
do so by the junior who had been instructed by a solicitor on the
Poor's Roll. Not only did Mackintosh not understand the language of the criminals but he had an erroneous idea of the
length of sentence which would make any impression on them.
In those days the friends and supporters of the criminals, particularly in Glasgow, used to occupy the public benches in the
balcony from which they shouted such comments as they could
before being ejected by the police when sentence was pronounced. Mackintosh's sentences tended to be grossly inadequate. This did not deter the supporters from shouting 'He's no
entitled to a' that' or 'Is there nae justice?' I fear that
Mackintosh took these remarks seriously even when he imposed
a sentence of three years' imprisonment on a criminal who
richly deserved ten years or more.

V   Silk (1959-1972)

As a silk the bulk of my work consisted of run of the mill reparation cases as it had done when I was a junior. In these cases I appeared both for pursuers and defenders. In the latter category Colvilles Limited, from whom I held a valuable retainer, figured prominently. In those days it was rare for a civil proof or jury trial to last for more than two days. They were frequently completed in one day. They are now often protracted by the lengthy and futile cross-examination of witnesses. It would be tedious to rehearse these numerous common-place cases. There were however some briefs which were of more than usual interest, at least to me. One of these was a case involving the question of the extent of the Lord Advocate's privilege.

The Lord Advocate's Privilege

It is trite law that the Lord Advocate enjoys absolute privilege in relation to acts done by him as public prosecutor (*Henderson* v *Robertson* (1853) 15 D. 292). The modern case of *Hester* v *Macdonald & Another* (1961 S.C. 370) demonstrates that this protection extends to Procurators Fiscal and their deputes when acting on the Lord Advocate's instructions and authority. I gained an intimate knowledge of *Hester's* case as counsel for the defenders and appellants in his action for damages for wrongful trial and imprisonment. The case had a remarkable genesis. Hester, having been charged with a crime on the Procurator Fiscal's petition in the Glasgow Sheriff Court, was granted bail by one of the sheriffs. In accordance with normal practice his address for citation and service of the indictment was, with the assent of his solicitor, agreed to be the sheriff clerk's office. For whatever reason, Hester never exercised his right to be liberated on bail. He remained in Barlinnie Prison as an untried prisoner until one morning when a warder told him, 'You're for the court.' 'What way am I for the court?' asked Hester. 'You're a production,' said the warder. He was then conveyed to the Glasgow Sheriff Court where he was placed in the dock of a court presided over by Sheriff E.O. Inglis (the father of R.A. Inglis, my contemporary at the Bar).

The case of *H.M. Advocate* v *Hester* was duly called in Inglis' court and, since he was unrepresented, the sheriff asked Hester if he pleaded guilty or not guilty. 'I havenae had an indictment' was the reply. The sheriff sought clarification from the procurator fiscal depute who produced an execution of service of the indictment. The fact that the indictment had been served at the sheriff clerk's office, where it had lain uncollected, and not at the prison was not then apparent. The sheriff, being satisfied that proper service of the indictment had been effected, told Hester, 'Quite frankly, I do not believe you.' A jury was accordingly empanelled and the trial proceeded. Hester was convicted and the procurator fiscal depute moved for sentence. Before passing sentence the sheriff asked Hester whether he had anything to say and again received the reply, 'I havenae had an indictment.' The sheriff then told him that, when he reached the place to which he was about to send him, he could make such representations as he saw fit to the Secretary of State. A sentence of imprisonment was then pronounced.

Finding himself back in Barlinnie to serve a term of imprisonment Hester sought legal advice. When investigation disclosed that Hester had indeed never received an indictment, the Crown ordered his immediate release. This did not satisfy the aggrieved Hester who raised an action for damages in the Glasgow Sheriff Court for wrongful trial and imprisonment against the Procurator Fiscal and his depute who had conducted the 'trial'. For the defenders it was pled that the action was irrelevant as the defenders were protected by privilege. However, the sheriff (N.M.L. Walker) allowed a proof before answer, that is to say an inquiry into the facts before deciding the issue of privilege. The sheriff's allowance of a proof was affirmed by the sheriff principal (Sir Robert Sherwood Calver, Q.C.). It was at this stage that I was brought into the case and presented the argument to the First Division of the Court of Session that the defenders were covered by the cloak of the Lord Advocate's absolute privilege with the result already indicated. The action was dismissed.

The Lyon Growled

In 1965 Dundas & Wilson who continued to enjoy the ancient designation of Clerks to the Signet, instructed me on behalf of their client Sir Hugh Lucas-Tooth, to advise as to what steps, if any, could be taken to enable him to secure a conditional legacy. The conditions were that he should assume the additional name of Monro of Teananich and matriculate the Arms of Monro of Teananich. Sir Hugh's original surname was Warrender. He inherited the baronetcy of Lucas-Tooth when a testator bequeathed to him a legacy on condition that he assumed the name and style of Lucas-Tooth, Baronet. He accordingly petitioned Garter King of Arms for recognition that he had succeeded to the Lucus-Tooth baronetcy. He thus satisfied the testator's conditions and became entitled to the legacy.

On being left the further legacy on condition of his becoming Monro of Teananich, Sir Hugh instructed Dundas & Wilson to present the necessary petition for matriculation of the Arms of Monro of Teananich to the Lord Lyon King of Arms (Sir Thomas Innes of Learney), which they did. However, Lyon, being displeased by the fact that Sir Hugh had applied to Garter in connection with the Lucus-Tooth bequest, failed to give a favourable response to Sir Hugh's petition to him to matriculate the Arms of Monro of Teananich. Sir Hugh was in despair as he was ageing and saw the prospects of his obtaining the legacy receding. What was he to do? I told him that the only possible course I could suggest was that, subject to the agreement of the testator's trustees, a special case on agreed facts should be presented to the Inner House of the Court of Session in which it would be submitted to the court that, as Sir Hugh had done everything he could to satisfy the conditions of the legacy, the condition that he should matriculate the Arms of Monro of Teananich had flown off and he was entitled to the legacy. I had some doubt as to whether this argument would succeed. Happily it was well received and Sir Hugh went on his way rejoicing.

When the result of the case reached the ears of Lyon he was not pleased. In the course of a fascinating letter to Dundas & Wilson he remarked that if another misguided testator were to leave a bequest to his client on condition that he called himself 'Snuggins', he would promptly do so.

Tam Innes was as striking in appearance as he was in speech.

He was a tall, lanky figure with long white hair. He spoke the Doric in a high-pitched voice. At a bar dinner he set himself on fire through causing his white locks to come in contact with a candle while making a speech. Thus it was said that the Lyon's mane was singed.

When the late Lord Airlie telephoned Innes early one morning he said 'It's Airlie here.' 'It's airly here too' replied Innes.

The Loch Lomond Water Scheme

In September 1966 I appeared before Parliamentary Commissioners in Edinburgh to promote the Loch Lomond Water Scheme on behalf of the water authorities who were directly concerned. This was an extensive but basically simple scheme designed to augment the supply of water across practically the whole of the central belt of Scotland. The essence of the scheme was the control of the outflow of water from Loch Lomond into the river Leven so that the water in the Loch would be maintained at a constant level and that so much of the water that flowed out of the Loch as was surplus to river conservation would be piped into the water system serving the extensive area described. When I appeared before the Commissioners with Bill Walker (now W.M. Walker, Q.C., a National Insurance Commissioner) I was confronted by an array of objectors. In the van were a number of local authorities for whom Donald Ross, Q.C. (now Lord Justice-Clerk), James Mackay Q.C. (now Lord Mackay of Clashfern and Lord Chancellor) and David Hope (now Lord President) appeared. There could not have been a more formidable team. These local authorities sought to object to the scheme on the ground of a potential future liability to contribute financially to the scheme. I immediately objected to the relevancy of the objectors' case on the ground that they had no *locus* to object. This objection was sustained by the Commissioners. The result was that the objections were repelled without the hearing of any evidence and the Commissioners reported to Parliament in favour of the scheme.

I assumed that the success which I had achieved before the Commissioners was final. However, the astute counsel for the objectors discovered a procedure whereby the objectors could petition Parliament for a re-hearing before a Joint Committee of both Houses. This procedure was accordingly adopted by the objecting local authorities. Their petition was granted. The Joint Committee sat in a committee room in the Palace of Westminster. I again appeared for the promoters, on this occasion with Gerald Moriarty (now Q.C.) of the English Bar in addition to Bill Walker. By this time the Secretary of State for Scotland had interested himself in the proceedings and supported the promoters. He was represented by Kenneth Jupp, Q.C., of the English Bar (now a retired judge of the High Court) and Willie Prosser (now Lord Prosser). On this occasion the objectors' team of counsel was augmented by an English junior from the Parliamentary Bar. As the promoters had been successful before the Commissioners in Edinburgh, the onus was now on the objectors to displace the conclusion of the Commissioners. This they sought to do by leading technical evidence of an engineering and financial character. Kenneth Jupp substantially assumed the burden of cross-examination which he discharged very effectively. At the conclusion of the evidence adduced by the objectors the Committee retired for a short period. When they returned, the Chairman (Lord Royle) announced that, without calling on the promoters to lead evidence, they were satisfied that the conclusion reached by the Commissioners in Edinburgh could not be disturbed. In accordance with parliamentary practice, no reasons were given.

1967-1968

My civil practice continued to flourish but in 1967 my wife became mortally ill and died on 7 March 1968. My four daughters had immediately recognised their mother's fate when they saw her in hospital in 1967 and displayed remarkable fortitude. After Josephine's death I received enormous support from my professional brethren and, in particular, from Lord Kilbrandon, from Bill and Margo Hook and from George and Lils Emslie who all provided me with boundless hospitality when I was lonely and at a low ebb. George was Dean of Faculty, an office which he filled with outstanding distinction. He led the Bar with the utmost style and ability. He had a smart military bearing which accorded with his distinguished war-time career in the army. He had passed the Staff College and had become a brigade major. There can be little doubt that if, at the end of the war he had chosen to make the army his career, he would have risen to the top.

At the end of May 1968, just after the office of part-time Sheriff Principal of Dumfries and Galloway had become vacant I met George Emslie one morning on my way up to the Parliament House. I said to him that I assumed that Donald Ross, who had been elected Vice-Dean of Faculty, would be appointed to that office. George with an unmistakeable twinkle in his eye replied that I was wrong. I then knew that I was to be the new Sheriff Principal of Dumfries and Galloway.

In the summer of 1968 I was invited for the first time to play in the annual golf match against the English Bench and Bar, played in alternate years at Woking and Muirfield. Thereafter I played regularly in this match until I retired from the Bench. These matches were most agreeable and convivial occasions. I enjoyed particularly the company and lightning wit of Charles Russell, who, on his appointment as a Lord of Appeal in Ordinary, became the third Baron Russell of Killowen. Although we had been connected by marriage for many years (his cousin Joan was married to my cousin Charles Brand), I did not meet him until the golf match of 1968. We then became fast friends. Charles was a man of immense charm, elegance and intelligence.

The Russells of Killowen were a remarkable legal dynasty. The first to achieve distinction in England was Charles' grandfather who began his professional life as a solicitor in Ireland. Thereafter he joined the English bar and became Lord Chief Justice of England. His son, Frank, who was Charles' father, also went to the bar and became a Lord of Appeal in Ordinary. Portraits of both Charles and his father adorn the Garrick Club.

VI   Sheriff of Dumfries and Galloway (1968-1970)

My two years as part-time Sheriff Principal of Dumfries and Galloway were the most enjoyable and satisfying years of my professional life. Not only did I and my daughters receive generous hospitality from the Lords Lieutenant of Dumfries, the Stewartry of Kirkcudbright and Wigtownshire on the occasion of my installation but in court I enjoyed the invaluable assistance provided by the able, educated and knowledgeable advocacy of the members of the local faculties. In Dumfries some of the older solicitors and others recounted kindly memories of my father. In Stranraer we enjoyed the delightfully happy and informal ambience provided by Lord and Lady Stair and their young children at Lochinch Castle.

Dumfries was by far the busiest court but George Carmichael, who looked after the courts in Galloway as Sheriff-substitute of the Western Division of the Sheriffdom following the death of Sidney Lockhart, was always ready and willing to help out in Dumfries, despite his tenuous hold on life due to congenital cardiac disease. George was an able lawyer and charming companion. His gallantry after Normandy had been recognised by the award of the Military Cross when, as a subaltern he found himself in command of what remained of a battalion of the King's Own Scottish Borderers. Unhappily, he died in the summer of 1970 while on holiday with his wife Ruth and their small son in Machrihanish.

After our marriage on 7 April 1969 Vera and I were presented with a handsome wedding present in the form of a silver sauce boat by the Faculty of Procurators of Dumfriesshire. Since she had been Josephine's bridesmaid at our wedding on 5 August 1948, Vera had been married to Tom Lynch of Beechmount, Mallow, County Cork. He died suddenly of a coronary thrombosis in 1958.

At the time of my appointment as Sheriff Principal, the Sheriff-substitute in Dumfries, who had been the Procurator Fiscal in Glasgow, proved to be incapable of dealing efficiently with any substantial litigation, whether civil or criminal. It subsequently

Wedding Day, 7 April 1969
the author and Vera

transpired that he was suffering from a progressive cerebral disease. In the result I had to reverse his decisions in some civil cases and take all the criminal trials on indictment myself other than those which George Carmichael was available to take. After about a year the Sheriff-substitute in Dumfries retired on the ground of ill-health and was replaced by Gordon Nicholson, a competent member of the bar.

As Sheriff Principal of Dumfries and Galloway I was an *ex officio* trustee of Ellisland on the outskirts of Dumfries. This was Robert Burns' home during the latter years of his life.

In those days the Sheriff Principal was the returning officer for all constituencies in his sheriffdom. As the Returning Officer the Sheriff Principal bore the legal responsibility for the proper conduct of the elections held in his sheriffdom but the Sheriff Clerks did the practical work of making the formal electoral arrangements. On polling day I toured the polling stations until the poll closed. As it was obviously impracticable for me to oversee the counting of votes and to declare the results in both Dumfries and Galloway, I delegated the responsibility in Galloway to George Carmichael. That was the position when the General Election of 1970 took place. In Dumfries I was extremely fortunate in having as Sheriff Clerk, Davidson, a man of incredible efficiency. In the result, although the Dumfries constituency embraced not only the burgh but also the widespread county, we were the first constituency in Scotland to declare the result. This I did on the steps of the Dumfries Academy at or about midnight, declaring Hector Munro to have been elected as the member for Dumfries in 1970. Since the reorganisation of local government the sheriffs have been replaced as Returning Officers by Chief Executives – a pointless change which has done nothing to improve efficiency but has derogated from the traditional status of a sheriff.

After the declaration of the result of the poll Vera and I returned to the Station Hotel, Dumfries, where we watched further results on television until it was clear what the outcome would be. Our pleasure at the results was not unalloyed because we had both formed a considerable affection for Dumfries and Galloway and we knew that, if the Tories were successful, I was likely to be invited to become Solicitor-General for Scotland, the acceptance of which would end my official relationship with the Sheriffdom. By the time we went to bed it was clear that the Conservatives were going to achieve a comfortable victory. On the following day somewhat reluctantly we drove back to Edinburgh.

Norman Wylie, Q.C., who had retained his seat as member for Edinburgh Pentland and who had been Solicitor-General in the last Conservative Government when Ian Shearer was Lord Advocate, was now appointed Lord Advocate. He asked me if I would accept office as Solicitor-General. I agreed to do so, provided it was understood that I could not serve in that office for more than two years as the salary was quite inadequate. I had begun the week following the General Election by carrying on my practice but, when I came out of court on the Tuesday, I was warned to stand by for a telephone call from Downing Street. Shortly after I reached home from the Parliament House the telephone call came from Edward Heath, the new Prime Minister. He invited me to become Solicitor-General for Scotland and I accepted his invitation.

VII Solicitor-General for Scotland (1970-1972)

Norman Wylie and I were formally installed in our respective offices before the Lord President and the other judges of the First Division of the Court of Session and I presented my Commission as Solicitor-General in the High Court of Justiciary. On 1 July 1970 we attended a dinner at No 10 Downing Street, the occasion being the eve of the opening of Parliament. The dinner was attended by all members of the Government plus the speaker of the House of Commons (Selwyn Lloyd) and the Secretary to the Cabinet (Sir Burke Trend). I was in the comparatively rare position of being a member of the Government without being a member of either House of Parliament. In the event this arrangement proved satisfactory as I was able to attend to the Crown Office side of the law officers' work in Edinburgh without having to be in London for parliamentary divisions. I was also available to appear for the Crown in both civil and criminal cases. At the same time I was kept au fait with Government business by attending the weekly meetings of Scottish ministers at Westminster when Parliament was sitting and collaborating with Norman Wylie in the Scottish law officers' chambers which were then in Dean's Yard close to Westminster Abbey. We were greatly assisted by the able and conscientious Joe Moran who was the number two on the permanent staff of the Lord Advocate's department. Unfortunately Joe had a very delicate constitution and died shortly after being promoted to be head of the department.

On U.K. problems Norman and I collaborated with Peter Rawlinson and Geoffrey Howe, the English law officers. Peter was a distinguished Attorney-General who was expected to succeed Hailsham as Lord Chancellor. Hailsham had gone so far as to secure the enactment, for the avoidance of doubt, that a Roman Catholic could be Lord Chancellor. He would certainly have graced the Woolsack but he never became a member of Mrs Thatcher's Cabinet. In the parlance of the day, he was a 'wet'. Geoffrey was an extremely able and industrious lawyer but, when Mrs Thatcher became Prime Minister, he joined her

The Scottish law officers following their installation, 1970
L: Lord Advocate, (N Wylie, Q.C.) R: Solicitor-General (the author)
(Scotsman Publications Ltd)

Cabinet as Chancellor of the Exchequer and was thereafter Foreign Secretary. Towards the end of his long tenure of the Foreign Office his views and those of the Prime Minister increasingly diverged. The situation culminated in his demotion to the office of Leader of the House of Commons coupled with the title of Deputy Prime Minister and, ultimately, his resignation from the Government. In my opinion Geoffrey was basically a lawyer rather than a politician. I regret that he did not stick to the law. He could have discharged the duties of any of the highest judicial offices with distinction. At the dinner in Downing Street on 1 July 1970 my eye was caught by the golden head of a young lady who was the only lady in the room. That lady was Mrs Margaret Thatcher and that was the first occasion upon which I had ever seen her. In point of fact she was not very young but had a fresh complexion and youthful appearance. I cannot remember having any conversation with her.

During my time as Solicitor-General, in addition to being responsible for the routine business in the Crown Office and leading for the Crown in a number of murder trials, criminal appeals and revenue appeals, I had to lead the bulk of the evidence at the fatal accident inquiries into three major disasters. These were the Ibrox Stadium disaster which occurred on 2 January 1971 and resulted in the deaths of 66 people; the Clarkston disaster which occurred on 21 October 1971 and caused the deaths of 21 people; and the Cairngorm disaster which occurred on 20 November 1971 and resulted in the deaths of six schoolchildren.

Three Major Tragedies

> *Sunt lacrimae rerum et mentem mortalia tangunt*
> Tears are shed for the world's distress and mortal affairs
> disturb man's mind
> Virgil: *Aeneid* Book I

The Ibrox Disaster

The Ibrox Inquiry was held in Glasgow before Sheriff Principal A.G. Walker, Q.C. (subsequently Sir Allan Walker, Q.C.) and a jury. W.I. Stewart, Q.C. (now Lord Allanbridge) who was then the Home Advocate-Depute and Donald Booker-Millburn (now a Sheriff of Grampian) appeared with me for the Crown. The relatives of the deceased, the Rangers Football Club and the Glasgow Corporation were all separately represented by counsel. It was an extraordinary phenomenon that 66 spectators were killed within a matter of minutes through falling on top of each other. The jury found that in each case the cause of death was asphyxia caused by overwhelming pressure in stairway 13 at Ibrox. The jury also found that the evidence suggested that a possible cause of the accident may have been that one or more persons fell or collapsed upon the stairway at a time when those descending the stairway were packed closely together, and were being pushed downwards by the presence of those above and behind them. The downward pressure of the crowd above forced other persons to fall or collapse upon those who had fallen first, and, as the downward pressure continued, more and more persons were heaped upon those who had fallen, or were pressed hard against them. This process was not halted before the deaths and fatal injuries had occurred. The jury also found 'That deaths or injuries will always be liable to occur in this stairway in its present state if a densely packed mass of people has been allowed to descend the stairway'. The jury found 'That (a) reduction in numbers using the stairway is a matter for expert advice; the jury recommends (b) that expert advice also be sought generally on methods of egress from football grounds'.

The Ibrox Inquiry had been preceded by a very thorough police investigation conducted under the direction of Detective Superintendent Beattie. That investigation entailed the taking of statements from over 1000 witnesses. The number of spectators who attended the match was about 80,000. The evidence was that they were well behaved. A Committee under the chairmanship of Sir John Lang had recommended a ratio of one police officer per 1000 spectators for crowd control.

At Ibrox the number of police provided was 333 which was, of course, vastly in excess of that recommended. A few of the constables had been detailed to perform 'close patrol' at specified times. I was mystified by the expression 'close patrol'. It seemed to suggest a group of constables operating as a tight-knit unit. Far from that being the case it transpired that the duty of those on 'close patrol' was to prevent spectators from entering and urinating in the common entrances to neighbouring flats – an interesting social commentary!

The Clarkston Disaster

The Clarkston Inquiry was held in Paisley Sheriff Court before Sheriff Principal W R Grieve, V.R.D., Q.C. (subsequently Lord Grieve) in February 1972. The disaster was caused by the blowing up of a newly constructed shopping centre which had a car park on its roof on 21 October 1971. The jury found that 'the accident was caused as a result of gas escaping through a fracture in the four inch gas main, laid beneath the pavement in front of the shops at Clarkston Toll Shopping Centre, into the unventilated void below said shopping centre, which gas subsequently became ignited and exploded... It has been proved to our satisfaction that the gas main fractured as a result of stress and corrosion of the four inch gas main'. It appeared that the stress which contributed to the fracture of the gas main resulted from the instability of the ground on which it was laid. Why it was corroded was not explained. I assume that claims for damages at the instance of relatives of the deceased were made against those responsible for the gas main and that they were settled. I neither read nor heard any more of the matter. Before the Clarkston Inquiry had been concluded I had to leave the Crown representation in the able hands of Ian Stewart so that I could reach Banff in time for the opening of the Cairngorm Inquiry. Before closing my account of the Clarkston disaster, I must record that one of its victims was Etty Pattullo, the wife of Sheriff Pattullo, unhappily also now deceased.

The Cairngorm Disaster

The Cairngorm Inquiry was held in the Sheriff Court at Banff before Sheriff Principal Mackenzie Stuart, Q.C., (subsequently a Lord of Session and thereafter a judge and later President of the E.E.C. Court in Luxembourg). It lasted for six days and ended on 15 February 1972. This Inquiry was the most heart rending but also the most interesting of the three inquiries. It was heart rending because it demonstrated that the deaths of six schoolchildren should never have occurred. It was interesting because it proved that Cairngorm, if you accepted the evidence of Dr Adam Watson, to which I shall refer, is the most dangerous place in the world. The affair arose out of an invitation to the parents of children attending an Edinburgh Council School who were asked whether they would like their children to go on a weekend school outing to Cairngorm in November 1971. Not unnaturally, a number of the parents agreed, confident in the belief that their children would be properly looked after on the proposed expedition. In the event, the children were taken to Cairngorm by a girl aged 20 years, described as a physical education student, accompanied by a youth who had no apparent qualification. Having ascended to the limit of the ski lift the party set out to climb further thinking that, if the weather became unfavourable, they could obtain refuge in one of the high level bothies. In the event the weather closed in. There was a 'white-out'. Visibility was nil. In such circumstances, as was clearly proved at the Inquiry, the correct procedure is to stop and take advantage of any shelter that may be available until the storm has blown over. Instead of doing this, the party plodded on in the hope of finding a bothy. Even if they had found one it is doubtful whether the snow would have permitted entry. In the event, the whole party was exposed to the elements and six of the children died. In the course of the Inquiry I had the advantage of a most interesting conversation with Dr Watson, a distinguished naturalist and ornithologist to whom I have already referred. Dr Watson is physically a small person of slight build. He told me how he had lived among the eskimos and in Siberia and elsewhere in the harshest climates in the world but he had never come to harm. He also told me that of all the places he knew the most dangerous was Cairngorm because, throughout the twelve months, the weather there could change so suddenly, dramatically and unpredictably. I asked him how he accounted for his own survival. He attributed it to his observation of the birds. When he saw them taking cover, he did likewise. He stopped and took advantage of any dyke, bush or tree that he could see. He thought that the high level bothies were a snare and a delusion and should be demolished.

At the Cairngorm Inquiry it became painfully obvious that the unfortunate Edinburgh children had not been accompanied by any competent person. Their deaths should not have occurred. There must have been irresponsibility but, in a public sector enterprise such as state education, it is difficult, if not impossible, to know on whom to fasten the blame. It should be added that every year adults, notably English students, get lost on Cairngorm and other parts of the highlands and thereby expose not only themselves but also the members of the mountain rescue teams to grave danger.

A Notable Tax Case

The most celebrated civil case in which I appeared as Solicitor-General was *Allan's Trustees* v *The Lord Advocate as representing the Commissioners of Inland Revenue* (1971 S.C. (H.L.) 45) in the House of Lords. The Inland Revenue were holding the judgment of the Second Division of the Court of Session in their favour. The judgment in favour of the Revenue depended entirely on the difference between the English and Scottish law of trusts. If the trustees, the appellants in the House of Lords, failed, the result would be that, while the rate of duty on the estate would be 12% in England, it would be 70% in Scotland. This was a situation which I found wholly distasteful and tried to persuade the Inland Revenue to concede the appellants' case. To this the Revenue would not agree and so I had to defend the judgment of the Second Division in the House of Lords.

Harry Keith (now Lord Keith of Kinkel) appeared for the appellants and opened the case. Their Lordships appeared to be very unresponsive to Harry's submissions. My heart sank, particularly when my English junior, Jean Pierre Warner (now Warner, J.), whispered to me, 'We're winning.' My Scots junior was James Clyde (now Lord Clyde). I was called on to reply to Harry's speech and reiterated the argument which had found favour with the Second Division. At the end of the day the astute Lord Reid, who was in the chair, found his way round the problem by construing the Scots law of trusts in such a way as to ensure equality of liability to duty on either side of the border.

VIII *Outer House Judge (1972-1984)*

I received news of my appointment to the bench by telephone from Norman Wylie during the summer vacation of 1972 while Vera and I were staying with Bill and Margaret Grant in Sutherland. Bill was then Lord Justice-Clerk. Unhappily this was to be his last holiday but we had a very happy time. Bill and I played golf at Golspie in the mornings. In the afternoons we went through the motions of helping Margaret with her beloved garden which she formed out of what had been croft land. Their attractive house consisted of the old croft house which had been modernised and enlarged by joining it to what had been the barn and was now the drawing room.

The Death of Lord Grant

I was installed on the bench at the beginning of the winter session of 1972. A few weeks later Bill Grant was killed on a wet Sunday afternoon while returning by road from a visit to his aged mother in Keith. This was a tragic accident for the occupants of the north-bound car with which Bill collided as well as for Bill and his family. Bill's death was a serious loss to the bench. He had a brilliant mind. He had been Ronald Morison's devil and learned from that master of the art the principles of advocacy. The result was that he was impatient of counsel who did not present their arguments concisely and logically. On occasion his temper flared inappropriately and an apology followed. He was by nature kind and charming.

Reid was very keen that Bill should become a Lord of Appeal in Ordinary. He was in fact offered such an appointment while he was Lord Justice-Clerk but he was unwilling to leave Edinburgh and declined it. This happened while I was Solicitor-General. The one appointment Bill wanted was that of Lord President in succession to Hamish Clyde.

Clyde had been appointed Lord President following Cooper's resignation in 1954. Since his death Clyde has been traduced by journalists and others who have forgotten or never knew that his

The author and Vera with his four daughters following his judicial installation
(Beaverbrook Newspapers)

appointment had been welcomed as a breath of fresh air by many of the bar. Where Cooper fretted for days over developing administrative reforms to accelerate the disposal of litigation that did not work, Clyde made a few jottings on the back of a post card and communicated them to the officials. The same basic approach applied to their handling of appeals, whether civil or criminal. Cooper was obsessed by strict adherence to technical rules of procedure but Clyde, who had a more realistic understanding of criminal work, in particular, was only concerned that there had been no miscarriage of justice.

On a celebrated occasion after Cooper had declined an appointment to the House of Lords and had led the Court of Criminal Appeal to quash a conviction on the ground of a departure from what he considered to be correct procedure by the police, the late Jim Johnston (Sheriff Welwood Johnston, a son of Lord Sands) wrote to Douglas Campbell, Q.C., that, if Cooper had followed the path of duty he would now be enjoying the favours of the ladies of Jermyn Street instead of hindering the Scottish police in the defeat of crime! The thought of Cooper trysting a courtesan makes the mind boggle!

The sudden death of Bill Grant urgently raised the question of who should be appointed Lord Justice-Clerk. It had hitherto been traditional that a serving Lord Advocate secured for himself any vacancy in the offices of Lord President or Lord Justice-Clerk or one of the two Scottish appointments of Lord of Appeal in Ordinary in the House of Lords. For example, Thomas Shaw and William Watson had gone straight to the House of Lords. Normand went directly from the Lord Advocateship to the Lord President's chair and Aitchison followed the same course to become Lord Justice-Clerk. Aitchison was followed as Lord Justice-Clerk by Lord Advocate Cooper before the latter became Lord President on Normand's appointment as Lord of Appeal in Ordinary. Cooper's successor as Lord Justice-Clerk was Alexander Moncrieff who was already in his seventies and had been on the bench for about twenty years. He had to resign within a year on account of angina. He was succeeded by George Thomson who was then Lord Advocate. Thomson, whom I have already described as a great judge, was modest and self-effacing but proved to be one of the outstanding judges of this century. It would accordingly have been in accordance with precedent if Norman Wylie had become Lord Justice-Clerk in succession to Bill Grant; but Norman was determined to break the tradition that the most senior judicial appointments were perks of the Lord Advocate and to demonstrate that they were uninfluenced by political affiliations.

There is no doubt that in bygone days the influence of politics on judicial appointments had, on occasion, been disgraceful. For example, Alexander Asher, a Liberal, was Dean of Faculty from 1885 until his death in 1905. Had he not been on the 'wrong side', he would unquestionably have been appointed to the bench. In fairness it must be said that Asher indicated that he could not have accepted a judicial appointment from a Tory Government. Both parties were equally culpable. Shaw of Dunfermline owed his elevation to the Lords to his arrival on Asquith's doorstep when he was in the middle of a case in the Court of Session and ought to have been in Edinburgh. Having learned of Lord Robertson's sudden death, Shaw had immediately taken a train from Edinburgh to London to press his claim to the resulting vacancy in the Lords.

On the death of Bill Grant the question was accordingly the stark one of who was best qualified professionally to become Lord Justice-Clerk. I had no doubt that the two best available judges were Ian Fraser and Jack Hunter, but Fraser had agreed to accept the next vacancy in the Lords which was likely soon to occur and Hunter had just succeeded Kilbrandon as Chairman of the Scottish Law Commission. In my view Fraser's prospective appointment to the Lords, for which he was admirably qualified, effectively excluded his appointment as Lord Justice-Clerk. Hunter, on the other hand, could readily have been promoted as there would have been no serious difficulty in appointing another Chairman of the Scottish Law Commission. He could have been replaced by Peter Maxwell, an exceptionally able lawyer with an original mind, who became Chairman of the Scottish Law Commission some years later in succession to Hunter. Hunter would have made a first class Lord Justice-Clerk. He had proved himself to be a person of outstanding judicial calibre with a penetrating brain which he used with exceptional industry.

In the event, the appointment went to John Wheatley who

had been the senior member of the Second Division under Bill Grant. He had been a judge for about 20 years. Before his elevation to the bench he had been a Labour M.P. and had been successively Solicitor-General and Lord Advocate in the Attlee government. His appointment to the Justice Clerkship by a Conservative government could not therefore be criticised on political grounds. It was, however, open to question whether he was temperamentally suited to the office.

Wheatley was a kind and generous man. It was unfortunate that his judicial style, which displayed pedantry and didacticism, did so much to conceal a sterling character. When Wheatley had been Lord Advocate, Douglas Johnston was the Solicitor-General for Scotland. When Johnston died the *Times* obituarist observed that 'there were times when his patrician manner belied his political beliefs'. Wheatley was the converse. His populist image belied his public school education. During his years in the Outer House Wheatley proved himself to be a sound and industrious judge of first instance, but his judgments, which were verbose in the extreme, were sometimes expressed in terms which attracted unfortunate publicity. For example, in the Argyll divorce case (*Duke of Argyll* v *Duchess of Argyll*) in 1963, after referring to a submission by counsel for the Duchess that the period between 9 am and 10 am was an unlikely one for the committing of adultery, his Lordship said that since his elevation to the bench and 'after long experience' he had reached the conclusion that there were no prescribed or proscribed hours for the act.

Wheatley's sermons to criminals provided the press with useful copy. His 'adumbrations', 'animadversions' and references to 'condign punishment' became notorious. Having cultivated the cloth cap image of the Shettleston boy, he thought he understood the mentality of the Glasgow criminal which he did not. As chairman of the First Division Hamish Clyde got to the point in half the time and was more often right although more often criticised than Wheatley in the Second Division.

When George Emslie succeeded Clyde he soon proved himself to be an outstanding Lord President. He was patient, pre-eminently judicial and concise.

Life in the Outer House

In his Hamlyn Lectures Kilbrandon described the civil jury as 'a Bingo Session'. My own experience at the bar led me to believe that this derisive description of what was supposed to be a judicial process was not unfair. There was an invincible bias in favour of the 'poor workman' who had been injured, whether through his own fault or not and in favour of the widow even though her late husband had been the author of his own fate. By statute all claims for damages for personal injuries were to be tried by jury unless one side or the other (generally the defender) satisfied a Lord Ordinary in the Procedure Roll that there was special cause for withholding the case from a jury trial. In that event the case went to proof before a judge sitting alone.

The verdicts of civil juries were so notoriously unsound that the majority of the judges increasingly found 'special cause' for withholding claims for damages from jury trial. In the result by the time I went on the bench the civil jury had almost been killed off. This, as I soon discovered, was unfortunate for two reasons, namely (1) civil juries had become judicially minded and ceased to return verdicts based on pure sympathy; and (2) the Outer House judges, instead of having merely to charge a jury and receive their verdict, had to undertake the boring and laborious task of writing a judgment which, unlike the jury's verdict, could be subjected to a nit-picking analysis on appeal.

After I went on the bench, although there were not many cases sent for trial by jury, I did take a few. In none of them did the jury return a verdict with which I disagreed. My conclusion is that it is unfortunate that trial by jury in civil causes has been practically eliminated. I am in favour of the involvement of the layman in the administration of justice so far as practicable. I fear that, if there is no such involvement, the layman will become increasingly suspicious of the objectivity of the legal profession and, more importantly, of the bench. It is ironical that it has never been seriously suggested that the jury should be eliminated from criminal trials which frequently raise issues at least as complicated as those which fall to be determined in civil causes.

As a judge of first instance there were two judges whom I endeavoured to emulate. These were John Carmont and Ian

Fraser. They had both had very large and specialised practices at the bar. Carmont wanted more than anything else to go to the House of Lords as a Lord of Appeal in Ordinary but he was never offered a vacancy. Carmont was the leading counsel in shipping cases when they were a fertile source of litigation. In private life Carmont was the mildest and gentlest of men. Ironically, his fame as a judge sprang from his suppression of the Glasgow razor slashers. My experience of prosecuting before Carmont demonstrated that he was scrupulous in ensuring that an accused's defence was fairly and fully presented. But, if convicted, he would receive a severe sentence. Carmont had the same type of practice at the bar as Patrick Devlin had in England, far removed from crime, but they both proved to be first class criminal judges.

Ian Fraser had been elected Dean of Faculty in 1959 after a three-cornered contest. The other candidates were Ian Shearer (subsequently Lord Avonside) and Harold Leslie (subsequently Lord Birsay and Chairman of the Land Court). After he had been elected Dean, Fraser was invited to become Lord Advocate. He, self-effacingly, declined the invitation because of his regard for the Faculty who had elected him to be leader of the bar. I cannot remember how I learned that Ian had been offered the office of Lord Advocate and that he had declined it but I referred to it when I wrote to him on his elevation to the bench. He replied that he did not know that anyone knew about it and asked me not to disclose it, which I did not do until after his death.

Ian was a superb judge. He was wholly judicial but not as taciturn as Fred Strachan. Ian never sought to influence a jury in any direction. He thought, rightly in my opinion, that any such exercise on the part of the judge would be likely to be counter-productive. Ian went from the Outer House to the Second Division of the Inner House from which he was elevated to the House of Lords as Lord Fraser of Tullybelton. He was a very highly respected member of the Appellate Committee of the House of Lords. Unhappily, he was killed in a road accident caused by a sudden snowstorm while driving back to Tullybelton shortly after he had retired.

When I first became a judge there was an impressive array of talent at the senior bar which included Donald Ross, who was

Dean of Faculty, Peter Maxwell, Charles Jauncey and James Mackay, now Lord Chancellor. Peter Maxwell and Charles Jauncey were particularly helpful. They presented their arguments with the utmost clarity and precision. At the bar I had known them both very well and appreciated their outstanding abilities and total integrity. In 1969 when Charles and I were preparing to appear against each other in the House of Lords in *Devine* v *Colvilles Ltd* (1969 S.C. (H.L.) 67), an authority on the doctrine of *res ipsa loquitur*, Charles asked me whether I had considered the decision of the Australian Supreme Court in *Mummery* v *Irvings Proprietory Ltd* ((1956) 96 C.L.R., per Dixon, C.J., at pp.114 *et seq.*) which was very much in my favour. I had never heard of it but, having read it, realised how potentially important it was. When *Devine* came on in the Lords I referred their Lordships to the Australian case and told them that it was only through the kindness and professional integrity of my learned friend that I was able to refer them to it. Regrettably, none of their Lordships referred to the Australian case in their speeches.

Under our system of pleading it is impossible to exaggerate the importance of the assistance given to the bench by counsel. The system is frequently described as 'adversarial'. That adjective suggests that counsel for any party is engaged in a contest in which his primary concern is to win. That is a false concept. The primary duty of counsel is to the court and to the administration of justice (see *Batchelor* v *Pattison and Mackersy*, (1876) 3 R 914). It follows that counsel should cite all relevant authorities regardless of whether they support his submissions. (see my observation on the office of Advocate-Depute *supra*).

IX *Inner House Judge (1984-1989)*

I had a relatively long stint of just over 12 years in the Outer House of the Court of Session. In those days judges progressed from the Outer to the Inner House by seniority and not by selection. When my turn came I was fortunate in gaining a seat in the First Division presided over by George Emslie as Lord President and Lord Justice-General. I never disagreed with him or had cause to do so. He was a wonderful man with whom to work. Whenever we finished hearing an appeal, the three of us decided whether we were agreed on the result. If we agreed – and I cannot remember any occasion when we were not – George would say that he would draft an Opinion of the Court which he would circulate for our comments or he would ask one or the other of his two brethren to draft the Opinion of the Court.

As a member of an appellate tribunal the only occasion on which I felt constrained to deliver a dissenting opinion was when I was sitting with Lord Justice-Clerk Wheatley and Lord Stott in the case of *Young* v *Guild* (1984 S.C.C.R. 477). In that case the appellant had been charged with assault. The assault was spoken to in evidence for the Crown and was denied in evidence by the appellant and his wife. The prosecutor did not cross-examine the appellant or his wife. The sheriff accepted the Crown witnesses, rejected the defence evidence and convicted. It was held by the Lord Justice-Clerk and Lord Stott that the failure to cross-examine did not bar the prosecutor from seeking a conviction and the appeal was dismissed. In my dissenting opinion I said, 'I am of the opinion that, where the accused gives evidence specifically denying the charge made against him in his evidence in chief, the prosecutor must be assumed to accept the veracity of the substance of that evidence if he does not challenge it by cross-examination. It follows that, if an accused has given evidence which is wholly exculpatory, the prosecutor cannot subsequently ask for a conviction unless he has cross-examined the accused on the material parts of his evidence in chief. To sanction the course adopted by the prosecutor in this case would be likely to lead to unfairness by misleading accused persons and their advisers as to the position being taken up by the Crown and as to the need or otherwise to lead further witnesses for the defence.'

During my time in the Inner House the volume of criminal appeals became so large that George Emslie in his capacity as Lord Justice-General decided that, in order to keep abreast of the work, an additional criminal appeal court should be instituted. This was generally presided over alternately by Norman Wylie, who was a member of the Second Division, and by myself. This extra criminal appeal division normally sat every third week during session, that is, when the normal criminal appeal courts presided over respectively by the Lord Justice-General and the Lord Justice-Clerk were engaged on civil business, and for one week a month during vacation.

When I went on the bench I intended to retire as soon as I had served 15 years, the statutory period for a judicial pension, namely in 1987. However, George Emslie, who knew of my intention, persuaded me to postpone my retiral until he retired. I was then asked to stay on for a further term to give any help I could to the new Lord President, David Hope. To ensure my availability in the First Division during this period I was taken off the roster for criminal trials. I eventually retired on 31 December, 1989 having served five years in the First Division and a total of 17 years on the bench.

The years in the Inner House were my happiest on the bench. The appellate work was more interesting and less laborious than the cases heard at first instance in the Outer House. Also, there was the stimulating experience of discussing points of interest or difficulty with one's brethren. I have already expressed my high regard for George Emslie as Lord President and Lord Justice-General. During the term that I sat with him I formed an equally high regard for his successor. It did not surprise me in the least that David Hope immediately demonstrated the highest judicial ability when he took the Lord President's chair. He had been an outstanding Dean of Faculty, a supreme example of the iron hand in the velvet glove. He combined immense charm with an equal strength of character. As Lord President, he followed the pattern set by George Emslie in relation to the writing of opinions. The judgment of the court was thus normally embodied in a single opinion of the court, duplication of effort was avoided and the scope for debate as to the construction of the judgment as an authority in future cases was restricted.

There was criticism of Hope's appointment in some quarters on the ground that he lacked judicial experience. In my opinion this criticism was misconceived. In the past, as already indicated, it had been the normal practice to appoint a Lord President, or Lord Justice-Clerk directly from the bar. In my opinion it is desirable that a candidate for these offices should be appointed before the freshness and sharpness of his approach have been blunted by service in the Outer House.

When I came to the bar in 1948 all the judges, including the Lord Justice-General and the Lord Justice-Clerk, took their share of criminal trials. I well remember Cooper firmly directing the jury in what became known as the Temple murder in about 1952 that their verdict must be either guilty of murder or an acquittal after the Dean of Faculty (Cameron) had suggested that culpable homicide might be an appropriate verdict. Cooper was then Lord Justice-General. As capital punishment was then the mandatory sentence for murder, juries frequently sought refuge in a verdict of culpable homicide unless that course was firmly excluded. In the Temple case there were no grounds for reducing the charge on account of provocation or diminished responsibility from murder to culpable homicide.

When Hamish Clyde succeeded Cooper as Lord Justice-General, the practice of the Lord Justice-General taking trials himself lapsed and has never been revived. It is now inconceivable that he will ever again be able to take trials owing to the vast increase in the volume of administrative duties which have descended on him as Lord President and Lord Justice-General in addition to his onerous appellate work.

By the time I retired the legislature had provided for the re-employment on a daily basis of retired judges, provided they were under the age of 75 and had, in the case of Scottish judges, been nominated by the Lord President. The purpose of this provision was to provide a reserve of judicial manpower to relieve the increasingly serious problem caused by the mounting volume of business in the High Court and the Court of Session. Retired judges who were available for re-employment soon became known as 'mothballs'. I was happy to join their number and have regularly sat for approximately one week per month since I retired. In practice, mothballs are only employed on appellate work and never take the chair. In my opinion, this is a satisfactory arrangement. Work at first instance and especially criminal trials on circuit demand the services of relatively young judges who may be expected not to become over tired or impatient.

X   Criminal Trials

In the course of my judicial career I tried practically all types of serious crime and statutory offences, apart from treason. Many of these cases were sordid and some were pathetic. Occasionally, the criminals provided unwitting sources of humour. An example of the latter was the case of two men who, having been caught bringing a car load of controlled drugs from London while passing Lockerbie on the A74 road were placed in separate cells in Lockerbie police station. While in the cells they shouted to each other exchanging views as to what their stories should be. This interesting conversation was not unnaturally overhead and recorded by the police! They were tried in the High Court at Dumfries and convicted of possessing a large quantity of Class 'A' drugs within intent to supply them to others. They were clearly involved in the supply of dangerous drugs on a large scale. I imposed severe sentences.

Perhaps the most bizarre case with which I had to deal was that of a part-time fireman serving in the fire service in Grantown-on-Spey. He was arraigned before the High Court in Inverness charged with wilful fire raising. He pled guilty to the charge. The facts as narrated to me disclosed that he had set fire to property and then went to the fire station with all speed, raised the alarm and naturally became the first fireman available to attend to the fire. The story seemed wholly irrational but the reports laid before me disclosed not only that the accused was sane and fit to plead, but also that he was a man of impeccable character. I placed him on probation for a year subject to medical supervision and heard no more of the matter.

There were, inevitably, far more High Court criminal trials in Glasgow than anywhere else in Scotland. Consequently all the judges, apart from the Lord Justice-General and the Lord Justice-Clerk, found that they were each sitting in Glasgow on anything from one to four circuits per annum. We used to stay during the Glasgow Circuits in the Western Club in Royal Exchange Square but by about 1980 Bobby Johnston (Lord Kincraig) and I decided that, if the circuit judges could be provided with a government car and driver, we could spend our nights at home and the circuit life would be more tolerable. Bobby put up the proposal to George Emslie as Lord Justice-General who supported it and secured for us the car and driver. Thenceforth I never stayed overnight in Glasgow.

During the 1980s a majority of the Glasgow District Councillors expressed loud support for the freeing of the African politician Nelson Mandela who was then being detained by the authorities in South Africa. The District Council had re-named a square in Glasgow 'Mandela Square' and banners were displayed exhorting the freeing of Mandela. I learned that these sentiments did not commend themselves to a prisoner on trial in the High Court who inscribed on the wall of his cell, 'Fuck Mandela. Free me.'

The last case that I tried in Dundee (*Her Majesty's Advocate v Hunter*) was a murder trial which lasted for three weeks in July - August 1988. It was the most sordid and nauseating case that I can remember having to try. The Solicitor-General (Peter Fraser, Q.C.) led for the Crown. Lionel Daiches, Q.C., was the senior counsel for the accused. It was always a pleasure to have Lionel appearing as counsel. He was invariably concise, frequently witty and a very able criminal advocate. He certainly fully extended himself in the defence of Hunter, albeit unsuccessfully.

Hunter was convicted of murdering his second wife by strangling her with the lead of her dog, his first wife having committed suicide on account of his relationship with the woman whom he murdered. Hunter and his second wife, who were both social workers, were married on 1 November 1986. They lived in Carnoustie both before and after their marriage. She disappeared on 21 August 1987. The remains of her body were not found until February 1988. In fact Hunter had taken her with her dog to the vicinity of Melville Lower Wood, Ladybank, in Fife where he strangled her in his car with her dog's lead and then dumped her body in the wood. The dog's lead remained round her neck until her remains were found. Having committed the murder, Hunter drove away, taking the deceased's dog with him. Thereafter he stopped the car somewhere in Fife, removed the dog's collar which had two tags attached to it giving both his own address in Carnoustie and that of the deceased's parents in Glenrothes. Having removed the dog's collar he put the dog out of the car but retained its collar and drove off. The dog, which was elderly, was picked up as a stray and destroyed. Hunter took its collar home where it was ultimately found behind a linen basket.

Hunter put forward an elaborate alibi which began with his story that on 21 August, 1987 his wife had driven off by herself from Carnoustie to Dundee where they both worked, she being unwilling to wait even one minute for him. He said he thereafter went from Carnoustie to Dundee by bus. Initially, he thought that she had gone to her parents in Glenrothes to tell them of her pregnancy. She had, of course, not gone to her parents on that day and Hunter professed not to know what had become of her. The car was subsequently found in Manchester where it must have been driven by Hunter.

On some unspecified date before her death the deceased had told her sister, Sandra Cairns, that Hunter had said to her, 'It's you that should be dead and not Christine', Christine having been his first wife. He had also told Gillian Pelc, a house parent in the children's home where he was employed, that he was only marrying Lynda, the deceased, 'to screw up her life the way she had screwed up his.'

Significant evidence was also given by two prostitutes. One said that in June-July 1987, Hunter was having a regular relationship with her. The other said that in December 1987 Hunter took her to his house in Carnoustie. On seeing woman's shoes in a bedroom wardrobe this prostitute said that she asked Hunter if his wife was away. He replied that she was dead. At that date Hunter could only have known that she was dead if he had killed her as no one else knew she was dead until February 1988 when her remains were found.

Finally, in Glenrothes police station on 9 April 1988, Hunter said to Detective Inspector McPherson and Detective Constable Bramall, 'I feel I would like to tell you but it's past that now and I still have Colin (his son by his first marriage) to think of.' He then became a suspect and, having been cautioned at common law that he did not require to say anything but that anything he said would be taken down and might be given in evidence, he said, 'Yes, I've understood everything you've said. I know it looks black. I keep wanting to get it over with. It's been a long time but I can't, and who would believe me now?'

Hunter was duly convicted of murder and the mandatory sentence of life imprisonment followed. Thereafter he appealed against his conviction on the grounds that the evidence had been insufficient to entitle the jury to convict and that I had misdirected the jury. On 29 June 1989 the Lord Justice-General (Emslie) delivered the opinion of the court refusing the appeal.

A Glaswegian Epilogue

During 1989 I sat on the Glasgow Circuit for the last time. Among the cases on my list was that of a woman charged with possession of heroin with intent to supply it to others. In accordance with my normal practice in such cases I imposed a severe sentence. My macer, who was a tall, dark man of dour appearance, then led me off the bench. As we moved off I heard shouting and screaming from the body of the courtroom but could not make out what was being said. When we reached the judges' retiring room I asked the macer what all the noise was about. He replied, 'I fear, my Lord, that the lady whom you have just sentenced said you were a — old bastard.' Having disrobed me, the macer left the room but returned in a few minutes. 'I must apologise to your Lordship,' he said, 'It was not you that the lady said was a — old bastard but the gentleman for whom she was keeping the drugs.' On that not inappropriate note I bade the High Court in Jail Square, Glasgow, a final farewell. Some years ago 'Jail Square' became officially 'Jocelyn Square' but that cosmetic change has not altered the environment and the old name lives on.

XI *Laudator temporis acti*

The younger brethren inevitably ask 'How are things now (at the bar) compared to what you knew?' There are two contradictory but complementary answers. The first is 'Very different'. The second is, in the words of the Hodder Song, 'Ever the same but always new'. In his *Short Commentary on the Law of Scotland,* published in 1962, the late Professor T.B. Smith, Q.C., D.C.L., LL.D., F.B.A., wrote (p. 105): 'The Faculty nourished, and still preserves, a corporate spirit of its own – which is fostered by daily contact in the Parliament House and by the fact that practising members of the bar are expected to have an address within a particular area of the New Town of Edinburgh.' That statement accurately described the life and spirit of the Faculty, not only in 1962, but also when I was admitted in 1948 and during the preceding centuries. In his contribution to the *Dictionary of National Biography* on the life of Lord Shaw of Dunfermline, the first Baron Craigmyle, Lord Macmillan wrote: 'The generous and democratic fraternity of the Parliament House is always ready to extend a welcome to ability, however humble in origin, but at the price of conformity with its high professional standards.'

Legal Aid for the poor had existed in Scotland since 1424. Counsel and solicitors conducted 'poor' cases gratuitously until the Legal Aid and Solicitors (Scotland) Act 1949 came into force in relation to civil proceedings. The provisions relating to criminal proceedings did not come into force until 1964. The introduction of legal aid in civil causes did not have any noticeable effect on the life of the bar or its corporate spirit. It continued to be essential for any advocate who hoped to acquire and retain a practice to be in regular attendance in the Parliament House and to have an address in the New Town.

The effect of the introduction of legal aid in criminal causes, on the other hand, although not immediately apparent, was soon dramatic. For the first time in the history of the Scots bar it became possible for an advocate to live entirely on criminal work. Since most criminal trials were held on circuit, and particularly in Glasgow, an inevitable fragmentation of the bar resulted. There thus came to be a body of counsel who were hardly ever to be seen in Edinburgh and practically never in the Court of Session. Hamish Clyde when Lord President and Lord Justice-General from 1955-70 set his face against allowing the High Court to be in continuous session in Glasgow because he saw that such a development would damage the corporate life of the bar, but he was fighting a losing battle. The volume of criminal business has risen to such an extent that throughout the year there are now two to four judges sitting in Glasgow.

Another effect of the introduction of criminal legal aid has been to induce a number of solicitors who carried on litigation practices in the sheriff courts to transfer to the bar. They have thus learned that the demands of advocacy in the High Court are very much more onerous that those of the lower courts but the system of devilling does much to ease their passage.

The fragmentation of the bar might well have resulted in a disastrous erosion of professional ethics and standards of advocacy were it not for the continuing authority of the Dean of Faculty, the respect accorded to his office and the determination of successive Deans to maintain the highest standards of the Scots bar. It remains to be seen what the effects the decision to confer rights of audience in the higher courts on some solicitors has.

There is no doubt that it is now much easier for a newly called counsel to acquire a practice and to earn a substantial income than it was throughout the time that I was at the bar. This in itself carries the danger that a young advocate may be misled by his relative affluence into thinking that he has entered an undemanding profession and that he is more competent than in fact he is. Here again, the authority of the Dean and the occasional astringent comments of the bench have generally proved adequate to correct the gaucheries of the tyro.

Major improvements in the internal administration of the Faculty's affairs and finances and in the clerical and ancillary support for counsel have been introduced since I ceased to be in practice. As Clerk, and thereafter Treasurer of the Faculty from 1970-1977 David Edward (now a Judge of the Court of the European Communities) was a driving force in overcoming the traditional inertia of the Faculty in the conduct of its own affairs. The bar also owes a considerable debt to Donald Ross, both as Vice-Dean and as Dean, in introducing effective machinery to ensure, as far as practicable, that counsel receive the fees to which they are properly entitled. In my day the management of the practices of the entire bar was in the hands of four clerks who were determined to prevent any increase in their number. Since then Faculty Services Ltd has been incorporated and has assumed responsibility for the ingathering of fees due to counsel.

I cannot conclude this chapter without referring to a major change in the composition of the bar which has occurred since I was called, namely the admission of a considerable number of ladies. When I was called, Miss Margaret Kidd, as she then was, subsequently Dame Margaret Kidd, Q.C., was the sole female advocate. Since 1949 a trickle of ones and twos has swollen into a substantial stream. Margaret Kidd had been admitted to the Faculty in 1923 and was, I think, on her own until 1949 when she was joined by Isobel Sinclair. When Miss Kidd had been at the bar for some little time John Carmont was asked whether he had ever spoken to her. 'Well,' he replied, 'I've started to several times, but it's always turned out to be George Montgomery'! Montgomery was a gentle and timid man who eventually succeeded Candlish Henderson as Professor of Scots Law at Edinburgh University.

When Miss Kidd was joined by other ladies their steps were initially somewhat hesitant and their work was substantially restricted to divorce and the custody and aliment of children. But they soon demonstrated that they could compete on equal terms with their male colleagues. There are now several ladies in practice of outstanding professional ability.

It will be clear from what I have written that, compared to the Faculty which I joined, there is much that is new and very different. On the other hand, the fundamental standards of ability and integrity remain. There is one comparatively modern innovation which I do regret, namely the abolition of the requirement of qualifications in general scholarship in the regulations for Intrants to the Faculty of Advocates. In my opinion it is most desirable, if not essential, that a prospective advocate should have attained a reasonable standard of general scholarship. I am sure that the future of the bar is in safe hands. The younger members probably regard me as out of date and crotchety, particularly when I react to mispronunciations, split infinitives and grammatical solecisms which are now the common currency of the media and seem to be infectious.

The motto of the Faculty of Advocates, *'Suum cuique'* (to each his own), might be thought to be uninspiring and, possibly, suggestive of avarice but, on mature consideration, it seems to embody an appropriate ideal for a body whose purpose is to secure that justice is accorded to everyone. (See the article by Lord Hope in 1990, 35 Journal of the Law Society of Scotland 526). The cardinal rule of the advocate's profession is that his primary duty is not to his client but to the court and to the administration of justice (see the opinion of Lord President Inglis in *Batchelor* v *Pattison & Mackersy, supra*).

In *Right Ho, Jeeves*, P.G. Wodehouse said through the mouth of Bertie Wooster, 'One can't give the raspberry to a client.' Although he was referring to Gussie Fink-Nottle and not to a client, whether professional or lay, of a member of the bar, the observation is, in general, but not universally, applicable to the latter situation. Counsel must accept his client's story, unless it is palpably untrue, and he must pursue the remedy which his client seeks unless there is clearly no legal foundation for it. In the latter situation counsel must in the plainest terms advise the client that he has no claim in law. Such advice is generally accepted by the client but I have on occasion had to give a client 'the raspberry' by showing him the door when he not only refused to accept my advice that he had no claim but told me that I did not believe in justice.

XII *Postscript*

On 28 March 1994, at a meeting with the Chief Justice of Botswana in London, I was invited to become a Judge of Appeal of the Appeal Court of Botswana. This offer was accepted and in July 1994, together with my fellow Scot, Lord Wylie, I took the judicial oath in the High Court in Lobatse. We thus became two of the seven members of the Court of Appeal of Botswana which superseded the Privy Council as the final Court of Appeal in all causes, both civil and criminal, when Botswana (formerly the Protectorate of Bechuanaland) became an independent republic. The president of the court was Austin Amissah, a Nigerian. The other members of the court, in addition to Norman Wylie and myself, consisted of one from Ghana and three from the Union of South Africa. All business was conducted in English. Some of the counsel came from Johannesburg which was not far from the border. Hence the reason why the principal seat of the High Court was maintained in Lobatse and not Gaberone, the capital, which was some 60 miles away. Norman and I, as retired Scottish judges, were selected in order to preserve the Roman law tradition in the local law.

Despite the heterogeneous membership of the Court and of the bar, the proceedings were conducted smoothly and amicably. Apart from the occasional reference to a Latin tag, the influence of Roman law was not conspicuous. My lasting and happy recollection of Botswana is of a cheerful and friendly population and of a legal profession whose relationship with each other and with the bench was completely harmonious and free from any prejudice arising from race, colour or creed.

In Chapter IX I have recorded the fact that, before I retired on 31 December 1989, the only occasion on which I delivered a dissenting opinion was in the case of *Young* v *Guild*. I have now to record that, when sitting as a 'mothball' on 26 March 1993, under the chairmanship of Lord McCluskey, I dissented from the opinion of the majority in the case of *Connelly* v *Simpson* (1994 SLT 1096). *Connelly* was a claim for restitution. The

The full bench of the Appeal Court of Botswana, July 1994

pursuer claimed the sum of £16,000 that he had paid the defender for shares in a company called Comptel (Dundee) Ltd. The money was paid into the defender's personal bank account. At the time of the litiscontestation the shares had not been made over, and because of the defender having put Comptel (Dundee) Ltd into members' voluntary liquidation, they could not be made over. The Lord Ordinary (Cowie) in the Outer House (1991 S.C.L.R. 295) expressly applying the principle of 'restitution' allowed recovery. A majority of the Inner House decided that the claim failed. My dissent was expressed briefly: 'In my opinion the law is concisely stated in *Trayner's Latin Maxims* at p. 72, *sub nom Causa data causa non secuta,* where the learned author says "Money paid in purchase of a certain subject can be recovered on this ground, if the seller fail in delivery". That is this case.'

Although I may continue to serve as a 'mothball' for three more years, I will not irritate the reader with any further addenda.

Appendix

The Oration delivered by the Dean of Faculty (Cameron) at the Dinner held in the Parliament Hall to mark the centenary of the birth of Robert Louis Stevenson.

The Memory of Robert Louis Stevenson

Members of Faculty – This evening we as a Faculty are met together to recall the memory of one who left no mark in our legal history, no record in our voluminous reports, and no personal legend in this hall of forgotten footsteps; but however tenuous the link which binds Robert Louis Stevenson to the Parliament House, and however small the imprint which he left in this place, there is no room for doubt that in his life and in his work this Parliament Hall and its history left a deep and abiding memory.

This is neither the time nor the place for a literary assessment or appraisal of his rank in the hierarchy of letters, and I myself am neither qualified nor do I desire to undertake that task. For myself, apart from being incompetent, the effort would be, I think, irrelevant, if not indeed impertinent; but I venture to think it is both pertinent and relevant to dwell for a brief space of time upon the twin topics, related and associated, of Stevenson and the Law of Scotland. He at least, like so many of my brethren, knew enough law to distinguish between stillicide and emphyteusis. The one is not a crime nor is the other a disease!

He passed Advocate – I love the ancient phrases – on the 16 June 1875, and he left these shores for France in September 1875. There may be a connection! *[Laughter]* His practice was exiguous, as is that of many of us. It was limited, I believe, to four complimentary but adequately feed petitions, and his personal distaste for the honourable calling to which he had been driven is very apparent both in his youthful and his later writings, because I am sure you will recollect what he said about this very hall in which we are met in essays written when he was still a very young man: 'A pair of swing doors gives admit-

tance to a hall with a carved roof' ('neath which I speak) 'hung
with legal portraits, adorned with legal statuary, lighted by win-
dows of painted glass and warmed by three vast fires' (that was
in 1875, when there was no National Coal Board). 'This is the
Salle des pas perdus of the Scottish Bar. Here, by a ferocious
custom, idle youths must promenade from ten till two. From end
to end, in pairs or trios, the wigs and gowns go back and forward. Through a hum of talk and footfalls, the piping tones of a
Macer announce a fresh cause and call upon the names of those
concerned. Intelligent men have been walking here daily for ten
or twenty years without a rag of business or a shilling of reward.
In process of time they may perhaps be made the Sheriff-
Substitute and fountain of justice at Lerwick or Tobermory.'
[Laughter]

That was what he wrote as a young man. In his maturer
years, when distance had perhaps lent enchantment to the view
and judgment had reinforced his original sentiment, he puts into
the mouth of Alan Breck the comment, when David Balfour announced his intention of adopting the honourable calling of
Advocate of the Scottish Bar, 'A weary trade and a blaggard
one forbye'. Straight from the heart!

You remember that distinguished citizen of East Lothian,
Andrew Dale, taking David Balfour to the Bass, said, 'I am no'
just exactly what ye would ca' an extremist for the law at the
best of times.' I think there are many of us who would agree
with the good Andrew Dale's sentiments today, yet is it not sur-
prising that the youthful distaste should be so marked? I took
the trouble to collate the date of Stevenson's admission to the
Faculty with the official reports, and I find it coincides with 2
Rettie. Some of you may have heard of it. I have it here.
[Laughter]

The Lord President was the Right Honourable John Inglis;
you can see him there on his portrait; the Lord Justice-Clerk, the
Right Honourable Lord Moncreiff, full of honours and
achievement, the orator of Scotland, the statesman of the middle
years of the nineteenth century; and I find on the right hand of
the great John Inglis the formidable figure of Deas, the
Perthshire farmer's son who made good and forced his way
through the press on to the Bench, and is yet, not merely a
painted figure at the end of this hall that you may see, but a leg-

end still remembered. And again, in the Second Division, on the right of the Chair, that gracious, graceful, learned figure, Lord Neaves, and the first Lord Ormidale. There are many of us who have affectionate and happy memories of the courteous, helpful, wise figure of the second Lord Ormidale.

I turn the page of the volume and I find Lord Advocate – Edward Gordon, and Solicitor-General – William Watson. You see him on the wall. His name is still with us. His family still walk the floor. *[Applause]* But not yet on the road to Tobermory! The Dean of Faculty – Andrew Rutherford Clark, and idly turning the pages of that volume I find, culled at random, these names which to us, who are of a younger and perhaps feebler generation, are those of giants – Asher, Balfour, Robertson, Trayner, Jameson, Fraser. If you pressed the matter a little further (I did not go very far, I went to the House of Lords Reports) you will find the famous case of Steuart of Murthly, one of the most romantic, and, if I may say so, amusing cases of the late nineteenth century; the story of the 'other world' of Edinburgh, so well known to 'Velvet Jacket', as Stevenson was known in that world.

It is not very far from Heriot Row to Elder Street, but what a world of difference there was. From the broad-cloth solemnity of the stately squares of Craig's 'New Town' you were plunged in a few steps into a vivid garish half-world of taverns and perhaps other and less reputable haunts, filled with drabs and doxies, thieves and knaves, and the Edinburgh eccentrics of the day – and you will find them all in 2 Rettie (House of Lords Reports).

The judgements in the case of Steuart of Murthly are dated but nine days before the admission of Robert Louis Stevenson to this Faculty. The law was very different in 1875, and so was the Parliament House. There were fewer reports. There were no All England Reports, thank God. *[Laughter]* There were few laws and still fewer Orders. Indeed, I do not think there was such a thing as an S.R. & O. in 1875. I wonder what will happen in 1975! There were practically no Jury trials, as the Lord President has reminded us in a recent judgment, and in those days juries were given an ample jurisdiction. They were allowed to miss the target by at least one hundred per cent before they could be regarded as perverse, *[Laughter]* and the Inner House, undeterred by the flicker of a Shavian eyelid, was permitted to apply its own common sense to the perjury of a knave and was not compelled to take the printed line as the last word upon truth and fact. Not only so, but fees were paid so often in cash, and with instructions, and last of all, there were no typists to make nonsense of our drafts.

It was a very different world, but the extraordinary thing – or perhaps it is not so extraordinary – was that Stevenson never felt or understood the fellowship of the Parliament House, the real brotherhood of the Bar, or shared that spirit which unites all members of the College of Justice from the senior judge on the bench to the newest joined apprentice in a W.S. office in an understanding that it forms part of a great and historic system, not merely of jurisprudence, but, I venture to think, of justice. *[Applause]*

It was not the Parliament House of 1875, with what in retrospect appear to us its giant figures, that made its impress upon Stevenson's mind. It was the Parliament House of a Hundred years before. He turned from the 'Penny Plain' of the mid-Victorian broadcloth to the 'Twopenny Coloured' of the eighteenth century brocade, and I wonder, members of Faculty, how far that interest which was aroused and which led to such major consequences was due to the accident of his entry to an exhibition of some portraits by Raeburn. You remember his essay in that slim volume, 'Virginibus Puerisque', on 'Some portraits by Raeburn'. It was written not long after he was called to the Bar. It was written in the autumn of 1876, and it is remarkable that three portraits in particular caught his imagination, and I would like, if I may, to refer very briefly to each one of these.

The first by right of seniority and right of quality is that of Robert McQueen of Braxfield, Lord Justice-Clerk. Of that he wrote, 'A portrait which irresistibly attracted the eye was the half-length of Robert McQueen of Braxfield, Lord Justice-Clerk…the tart, rosy, humorous look of the man, his nose like a cudgel, his face resting squarely on the jowl has been caught and perpetuated with something that looks like brotherly love.'

And from that I pass to Lord Newton, Charles Hay, that genial toper, as he said, 'just awakened from clandestine slumber on the Bench.'

Then I pass to the second Lord President Dundas, 'with every

feature so fat that he reminds you in his wig of some droll old
Court Officer in a nursery story book...the nose combining the
dignity of a beak with the good nature of a bottle.'

And they are all on our walls today. There is Dundas, beside
Robert Blair. It is a copy and not a very good one, but you can
see the droll fat face. There is Newton, recently brought back to
his home from exile in the northern regions of the Mound, and if
you go into the corridor you will see the 'tart face' of Robert
McQueen of Braxfield, the Lord Justice-Clerk.

It was Braxfield who made that vast impact on Stevenson's
mind which had such fortunate consequences, and it is perhaps
no accident that of the two figures from the Faculty of
Advocates who have made the most stir in the world of letters,
both should have been influenced and affected by the memory
of that great and controversial figure, Braxfield. Do not forget
that the youthful Walter Scott dedicated his thesis upon admission to Braxfield, and Stevenson, in that essay to which I referred, paid his youthful and earliest tribute to that figure.

But perhaps observing that this is not an occasion for contro-
versy and this figure still brings with it the echoes of old arguments and old antipathies, I had better endeavour to suppress
my own feelings in the matter. I will, however, say this: that
there is little room for doubt that in the glowing, vigorous canvas of Raeburn, with its gallery of eighteenth century figures,
Stevenson found the inspiration which led him in his turn to
paint his gallery, to which we owe so much. And from that perhaps half casual contact, there was sown, germinated, and flow-
ered, a seed which gave us a series of portraits drawn in firm
lines, with truth and accuracy, coloured by affection, instinct
with understanding.

Let me, if I may, for a moment recall one or two of these.
They are all legal figures. Take, first of all, Rankeillor, the
Writer of Queensferry. Have we not all come across Rankeillor,
prudent, cautious, humorous, rosy Scots writer, the man who
provided the nice little periphrasis for Alan Breck, 'Mr
Thomson', and in his humorous quality could not resist asking
when Alan said, 'I bear the King's name'. 'Humph, I have never
heard of a King Thomson'. *[Laughter]* How typical of some
W.S.

Then you have Charles Stewart, the half-tamed Highlander in

the High Street, who said to David Balfour, 'I'm a lawyer, ye see, fond of my book and my bottle, a good plea, a well-drawn deed, a crack in the Parliament House with other lawyer bodies, and perhaps a turn at the golf on a Saturday at e'en'. I would pretermit the last myself, and you recollect the reply of Charles Stewart, the writer, when he made application to the Lord Justice-Clerk of Scotland for leave to interview the witnesses and to see the accused in the trial of James Stewart, and all he got in 1751 was a recommendation to the Military Governor – a recommendation! – and Charles Stewart's Highland blood boils: 'The Lord Justice-Clerk of Scotland recommends!' If he had lived in 1950 the Lord Justice-Clerk, I doubt, would not even have recommended. Today he would have been bound by *Liversidge* (*Liversidge* v *Anderson*, [1942] A.C. 206), that Magna Carta of the dictator, and he could do no more than wag a monitory and declaratory finger in terms of the Crown Proceedings Act, 1947.

Then, if one moves one step further, you recollect the famous consultation at Inverary over a bowl of punch, a Faculty affair, in which Sheriff Miller, later to become Lord Glenlee and the predecessor of Braxfield in the chair which Lord Alness so long occupied, took charge over the steaming bowl and where he and his colleagues, Brown of Coalstoun, Stewart of Stewarthall, and himself, thought of the revolution that might be made in Parliament House by judicious handling of David Balfour's affairs. Have we not all heard echoes in the corridor and elsewhere of similar smooth cabals? It might be the Parliament House in the twentieth century.

And then you pass from the practising lawyer to a type that for so long was with us, what I might call the lawyer Laird, Balfour of Pilrig, just sketched in faintly perhaps with the etching pen, but how clear a picture of the cultured country gentleman who became a member of the Faculty of Advocates, almost, I had said, as a matter of course; a type that, alas, perhaps is not so much with us today as it was 50 years ago, but we can still recognise them.

Then, from the sketches, the kitcats, the heads and shoulders, you come to the full-length portrait of the lawyer statesman, Grant of Prestongrange, in full figure just as you see him in Allan Ramsay's portrait, the firm face, the statesmanlike air, and all the rich gravity of the eighteenth century. That was a portrait of Stevenson's maturity in 1887 in 'Catriona', and these sketches and portraits are just like the Raeburn portraits; they are instinct with life, and as when you go into the corridor just now, Braxfield is almost speaking to you in living welcome, so these figures step from the pages of the eighteenth century and walk beside us in the twentieth. I leave last of all the tremendous figure of Weir of Hermiston, scarcely a caricature, but almost a loving portrait in its somber magnificence of that dominant Braxfield.

What a gallery! If he himself did not enrich Scots law, there can be no room for doubt, I suggest, that both his mind and his work were alike enriched by his contact with the Law of Scotland and with its figures. So in turn the familiar figures of our domestic history, enlarged and illumined by an artist's hand, are by him painted on the wider canvas of literature which knows neither domestic bounds nor national frontiers. But I think one thing is quite certain, that Stevenson's own affections were never far away from the city of his birth and upbringing, and even from this centre of its legal system.

Do you remember in his Essay on Edinburgh he quotes the remark of an old battered seaman who said that his idea of Paradise on earth was 'The New Town of Edinburgh with the wind the matter of a point free'? Well, now, I often think of that phrase, and often I think that when the wind is northerly or north-easterly, one may suspect that the spirit of Stevenson may turn from that Pacific hillside where his dust is laid to the stormier hills of his own countryside, and must often scud on a favouring breeze to the Pier of Leith, perhaps in the creaking brig 'Covenant' of Dysart, master, Eli Hoseason, and bring him by way of the Figgate Whins, Silvermills and the Lang Dykes to Parliament House. And what would he find? No Charles II – removed by municipal vandals! Our late brother, Lyon Mackenzie, would have said something which was perhaps even more apt – but I won't quote it – to describe the municipal people that he had in mind.

There one can see, blown on a favouring gale, this spirit once again pass within those folding doors to hold communion with Forbes and Erskine, Dundas and Braxfield, and to hear again the clash of muskets as the Corporal's guard brings James More, that smooth-tongued knave, to Prestongrange's house, and catch the echo of the thunderous growls of Hermiston in the High Court just along the way.

I was looking the other night at a volume of poems by Neil Munro, and I could not help noting a few lines from a requiem he wrote on Stevenson, because Stevenson, the Parliament House, and the Western Highlands always seem to me to be linked together. He said this:

> So you are happed and gone, and there you're lying
> Far from the glens, deep down the slope of seas;
> Out of the stormy night, the grey sleet flying,
> And never again for you the Hebrides.

Don't let us forget it was Stevenson who wrote, 'Merry of heart, he sailed on a day, over the sea to Skye'.

It is curious, to digress for one moment, if I may, how the misty Isle of Skye has played its part in Scottish romantic literature. Remember how, the night before the Battle of Otterburn, Douglas dreamed a dream, 'I hae dreamed a weary dream, beyond the Isle of Skye; I dreamed a dead man won a fight, and that dead man was I.' In the clang and clash of battle the following day Douglas lay dead, but his war-cry brought victory in the moonlight.

Now, Stevenson himself could not avoid doing what we all do, exposing himself, and in David Balfour I believe he expressed that which he would have denied in 1875, his own ultimate personal dream, the lawyer Laird, 'Balfour of Shaws'. Do you remember the last two touching pages of 'Catriona?' I won't endeavour at this time of night either to quote or paraphrase, but just recall to the memory of each one those closing paragraphs – that is the evidence. There was the dream – the Advocate Balfour of Shaws, the dream that for him was never to come true, as so many dreams are doomed.

It is time now to close 2 Rettie and to turn again to 1950 Session cases, to say farewell to romance and hopes and dreams, but to pause for one moment to acknowledge a man whom in his day the law passed by but on whose imagination the Law of Scotland and the old Scots lawyers worked with such power and to such purpose that he has left to us, his brethren in the law, a legacy of portraits and of memories that time and ourselves will not soon or readily allow to fade, and so in the sonorous Latinity of Catullus' line, *Atque in perpetuum frater ave atque vale.*

My Lords, Ladies, and Gentlemen, members of Faculty, I ask you to rise and in silence to drink with me to the memory of Robert Louis Balfour Stevenson, Advocate.

Index

Advocate-Depute, 47-52
Aitchison, Lord Justice-Clerk, 9-10, 72
Alison, Arthur, KC, 31-2
Allan's Trs v IRC, 69
Allanbridge, Lord, 65
Alness, Lord Justice-Clerk, 37
Anderson, Lt. Col. JDC, 14, 16
Arbuthnott, Donald, 4
Argyll divorce case, 74
Argylls, 14
Army days, 11-25
Asher, Alexander, 73
Austin, Alfred, 32
Avonside, Lord, 51, 76
Baker-Carr, Maj. RMT, 14
Barry, RSM, 11
Basset, Bernard, SJ, 7
Benedictine School, Edinburgh, 6
Birnam, Lord, 36-7
Birsay, Lord, 76
Blades, Lord, 27-8
Booker-Millburn, Sheriff Donald, 65
Botswana, Judge of Appeal, 90-92
Braid Road, Edinburgh, 6
Brand, Cecilia, 31
Brand, Charles (cousin), 58
Brand, Charles (great-grandfather), 4
Brand, Charles (uncle), 5
Brand, Clement, 4
Brand, Francis, 4, 24
Brand, Harry (brother), 2, 6
Brand, Harry (uncle), 4
Brand, James, 4
Brand, Jane, 31
Brand, Josephine (nee Devlin), 25-6, 29-31, 57
Brand, Lulu, 31
Brand, Madeleine, 31
Brand, Sheriff James Gordon, 1-6
Brand, Stanley, 4
Brand, Willie, 2, 6, 31
Brand, Vera (nee Russell), 4, 31, 59-60
Brandon Street, Edinburgh, 31
Brittain, Eric, 19-20
Bruce, Brig. John (later Professor Sir), 24

Bull, Frances (mother), 4
Burnet, JR Wardlaw, KC, 9
Cairngorm disaster inquiry, 67-9
Calver, Sheriff Sir Robert S, QC, 54
Cameron, Lord, 35-7, 41, 43, 48, 80, 93-101
Cameron v Hamilton's Auction Marts Ltd, 44
Cameronia, SS, 16-19
Campbell, Douglas, QC, 72
Campbell, Gladys, 5
Campbell, Maj. WM, 5, 22-3
Carmichael, Sheriff George, QC, 59
Carmont, Canon, 6
Carmont, Lord, 6, 42, 75 6, 88
Carr, Bobby, 21
Charles George & Brand, WS, 5
Chiasson, Fr, 24
Childhood years, 1-6
Clarke, Trevor, 19-20
Clarkston disaster inquiry, 67
Cloete, Len, 22
Clyde, Lord, 69
Clyde, Lord President, 36, 70, 74, 80, 87
Connelly v Simpson, 90, 92
Cooper, Jack, 21-2
Cooper, Lord President, 36, 41-4, 50, 70, 72, 80
Cowie, Lord, 37, 92
Criminal trials, 82-5
Cunningham, Jeffrey, 27
Daiches, Lionel, QC, 83
Dean of Faculty, office of, 87
Devine v Colvilles Ltd, 77
Donald, Sheriff Douglas, 46
Doyle, Jimmy, 19-20
Duffes, Arthur, QC, 10
Duffy, Frank, QC, 49-50
Dundas & Wilson, CS, 55
Dunedin, Lord President, 33
East Africa, 16-17
Edinburgh University, 9-10
Edward, Judge David, 87
Elliot, Lt. Col FM, 14
Ellisland, Dumfries, 61
Emslie, Lady, 57

Emslie, Lord President, 28, 29, 57, 58, 74, 78-9, 83, 85
English, Maj. Tony, 22
Ervine-Andrews, Capt HM, 11
Eskgrove, Lord, 37-8
Faculty of Advocates, 88-9
Faculty Services Ltd, 88
Farrell, Fr, 24
Fiddes, Sheriff JR, 29
Firth, Ernest, 7
Firth, Fr John, SJ, 7
Fowkes, Maj. Gen, 24
Fraser, Peter, QC (later Lord Fraser of Carmyllie), 83
Fraser of Tullybelton, Lord, 73, 75-6
Galletly, Ski, 22
Gibson, Lord, 35-6
Glasgow Juridical Society, 27
Glasgow Sheriff Court, 44-5
Gordon, (Canon) Hugh, 16
Grant, Lord Justice-Clerk, 51, 70
Grant, Sheriff-Substitute (Inverness), 44
Gray, Cardinal, 4
Gray, Fr, John, 4
Grieve, Lord, 67
Guthrie, Lord, 28
Hailsham, Lord, 63
Heath, Edward, 62
Henderson, Prof. Candlish, KC, 5, 33, 88
Hester v *Macdonald,* 53-4
Hill Watson, Lord, 43, 49
HM Adv v *Hunter,* 83
HM Adv v *McCulloch & Mackay,* 39
Hodder Place, 2, 6, 7
Hook, Mrs Margo, 29, 57
Hook, Sheriff WT, 29, 57
Hope, Lord President, 17, 56, 79-80
Hope, Lt Col. AHC, 17
Horsfall, Sheriff Alastair, 50
Howe, Sir Geoffrey, QC, 63
Hunter, Lord, 73
Huntingdoun, Dumfries, 2, 6
Ibrox disaster inquiry, 65-6
Inglis, Sheriff EO, 54
Inglis, Sheriff RA, 29
Inner House Judge, 78-81
Innes of Learney, Sir Thomas (Lord Lyon), 36, 55-6
Jackman, Capt. James, 11-12
Jauncey, Capt. JH, 27
Jauncey of Tulliechettle, Lord, 26-7, 36, 77

Johnston, Lord, 74
Johnston, Sheriff Welwood, 72
Jubb, Advocate, 29
Jupp, Kenneth, QC (Mr Justice Jupp), 57
Juridical Library, 31
Jury trial, civil, 46-7, 75
Keith of Avonholm, Lord, 42
Keith of Kinkel, Lord, 69
Kidd, Dame Margaret, QC, 88
Kilbrandon, Lord, 34, 51, 57, 75
Kincraig, Lord, 82
King's African Rifles, 16-24
Kinross, Baron (Lord President), 6
Kinross, Lord, KC, 6
Kissen, Manuel, QC (Lord Kissen), 47
Knox, Msgr. Ronald, 8
Lang, Sir John, 66
Legal aid, 86-7
Lloyd, Selwyn, 63
Loch Lomond Water Scheme, 56
Lockhart, Sheriff Sidney, 59
Lovat, Shimi, 14
Lucas-Tooth, Sir Hugh, 55
Lunnan, Tony, 23-4
Lynch, Tom, 59
Macdonald, Lord Justice-Clerk, 32-3
MacEwan, David, 37, 41
MacEwan, Robin, 37, 44
Mackay, Lord, 37-42
Mackay of Clashfern, Lord, 56, 77
Mackenzie Stuart, Lord, 67
Mackintosh, Lord, 51-2
Mackintosh, Murdo, 39
Maclay, Murray & Spens Solicitors, 26
Macmillan, Lord, 86
Macvicar, Sheriff Neil, 29
Maxwell, Lord, 73, 77
Maxwell, Robert, 6
Maxwell-Witham of Kirkconnell, Robert, 6
McKechnie, Sheriff Principal Hector, QC, 44, 47
McQueen, Capt. David, 13
McWhannell, Gilbert, 27
Milligan, Lord, 35
Moncreiff, Lord, 32
Moncrieff, Lord Justice-Clerk, 6, 72
Monro of Teananich, 55
Montgomery, Prof. George QC, 88
Moran, Joseph, QC, 63
Moray Place, No. 38, Edinburgh, 31

Moriarty, Gerald, QC, 57
Morison, Sir Ronald P, 34, 70
Morison, Lord (AM), 34
Morison, Lord (TB), 34
Murder, capital and non-capital, 48-9
Murray, David King, (see Lord Birnam)
Murray, Sheriff, C de B, 45
Nicholson, Sheriff CGB, QC, 61
Normand, Lord, 72
O' Connor, Fr Edward, SJ, 8
O' Connor, Fr Frederick, SJ, 8
Officer-cadet, 11-13
Outer House Judge, 70-77
Patrick, Lord, 38
Pattullo, Mrs Etty, 67
Pattullo, Sheriff William, 67
Philip, Sir Randall, QC, 35
Prosser, Lord, 57
Queen's counsel, practice as, 53-8
Radcliffe, Lord, 34
Rae, Francis, SJ, 7
Randolph Place, No. 2, Edinburgh, 4
Rawlinson, Lord, 63
Reid of Drem, Lord, 27, 33-4, 69, 70
Reith, Douglas, KC, 28
Risk, John, 26-7
Risk, Ralph, 26
Risk, Tom, 26
Robertson, L de CF, Major, 11
Robertson, Lord, 38
Rose, Angus, 16
Ross, Lord Justice-Clerk, 56, 58, 76, 88
Ross McLean QC, Sheriff Principal, 48
Royle, Lord, 57
Rushbrooke, Col, 19
Russell, Lord Chief Justice, 58
Russell, Lord, 42
Russell, Sheriff AMG, 37-9
Russell of Killowan, Lord, 58
Sands, Lord, 72
Schooldays, 7-8
Scotcrest, Gullane, 5-6
SE Asia Command, 19-24
Shaw of Dunfermline, Lord, 73, 86
Sheriff of Dumfries & Galloway, 59-62
Simpson, TB, KC, 38, 45
Sinclair, Isobel, QC, 88
Skerrington, Lord, 5
Slayter, Maj. ELP, 14

Sloan, Norman, 37, 40
Smith, Professor Sir Thomas, 86
Solicitor General of Scotland, 61-2
Sorn, Lord, 51
Stair, Lord and Lady, 59
Stevenson, Robert Louis, 32, 37, 93-101
Stonyhurst, 6-8, 11, 13
Stott, Lord, 78
Strachan, Lord, 34, 76
Student days, 26-7
Taylor, AE, 10
Thankerton, Lord, 33
Thatcher, Mrs Margaret, 65
Thomas, Mabel, 4
Thomson, Lord Justice-Clerk, 27, 44, 72
Thurso boy inquiry, 50-52
Trayner, Lord, 32-3
Trend, Sir Burke, 63
Walker, George, 35-6
Walker, Lord, 35-6
Walker, Sheriff NML, 54
Walker, Sheriff Sir Alan, QC, 65
Walker, WM, QC, 56-6
Wallace, Sheriff Robbie, 35
Warner, Mr Justice, 69
Waterton, John, 8
Watson, Dr Adam, 68
Watt, Clifford, QC, 50
Wedderburn, Innes, WS, 9, 26
Weld, Thomas, 7
Wheatley, Lord Justice-Clerk, 73-4, 78
Whitehouse, Edinburgh, 4
Windebank, Mrs, 31
Wylie, Lord, 62-3, 70, 73, 79, 90
Young, Lord, 32-3
Young v *Guild,* 78-9